American Presidents' Wit and Wisdom

A Book of Quotations

Edited by Joslyn T. Pine

DOVER PUBLICATIONS, INC.
Mineola, New York

Bibliographical Note

This Dover Large Print Classics edition, first published in 2002, is an unabridged slightly updated republication in large print format of *Wit and Wisdom of the American Presidents,* which was originally published by Dover Publications, Inc., in 2001.

Library of Congress Cataloging-in-Publication Data

Wit and wisdom of the American presidents
    American presidents' wit and wisdom : a book of quotations / edited by Joslyn T. Pine.
       p. cm. — (Dover large print classics)
    Unabridged slightly updated republication in large print form of Wit and wisdom of the American presidents. 2001
    Includes index.
    ISBN 0-486-42469-3 (pbk.)
    1. Presidents—United States—Quotations. 2. United States—Politics and government—Quotations, maxims, etc. 3. American wit and humor. 4. Large type books. I. Pine, Joslyn T. II. Title. III. Series.

E176.1 .W835 2002
352.23'8'0973—dc21

2002074148

Manufactured in the United States of America
Dover Publications, Inc., 31 East 2nd Street, Mineola, N.Y. 11501

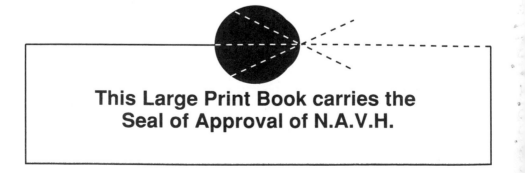

**This Large Print Book carries the
Seal of Approval of N.A.V.H.**

Note

"If men were angels," remarked James Madison in the 51st Federalist Paper, "no government would be necessary." This notion at least partially expressed the sentiments of the Founding Fathers as they sought to shape the government of the young nation at the Constitutional Convention in Philadelphia in 1787. Yet it is just as true to say that they were equally mistrustful of too much authority. Their ultimate solution, therefore, was to achieve a balance by defining a strong central authority that was limited in its ability to abuse power.

While constitutional provisions for the legislative branch are described in meticulous detail, the American Constitution is rather vague and ambiguous on the subject of presidential powers. Some, of course, are enumerated, such as the role of commander in chief of the armed forces, the authority to grant pardons and reprieves, the veto power over legislation, as well as the ability to make treaties with the consent of the Senate, and to appoint judges and ambassadors. In fact, as our history has unfolded, this lack of precise definition for the executive branch has been fortunate, since it has allowed the presidency to evolve both through circumstance and the particular nature of the individual at the helm. Those presidents held in highest esteem by historians, such as George Washington, Abraham Lincoln, Woodrow Wilson, and Franklin D. Roosevelt, filled the office when far-reaching powers were demanded in order for the nation to survive times of crisis. And in the spirit of these remarkable men—as well as the lesser lights, but lights nonetheless—history is truly biography as we reflect on the story of America as also the story of its presidents. Here, their own words mark the great themes in American history and also vividly reveal their personalities.

Since a wide variety of sources was consulted to compile these quotations, punctuation has, for the most part, been modernized and standardized for the sake of clarity and consistency. Chronological order was not an organizing principle here because many of the source quotes were undated. And since four different sources might each contain a different version of the same quote, every effort has been made to present the version closest to the spirit and substance of the original.

George Washington

Born February 22, 1732—Died December 14, 1799
1st President, 1789–1797 ★ Federalist

Discipline is the soul of an army. It makes small numbers formidable; procures success to the weak, and esteem to all.

Few men have virtue enough to withstand the highest bidder.

At a distance from the theatre of action truth is not always related without embellishment.

I hate deception, even where the imagination only is concerned.

It is not a custom with me to keep money to look at.

I hope I shall possess firmness and virtue enough to maintain what I consider the most enviable of all titles, the character of an honest man.

[attributed] Father, I cannot tell a lie. I did it with my little hatchet.

Labor to keep alive in your breast that little spark of celestial fire, called conscience.

Truth will ultimately prevail where there is pains taken to bring it to light.

A slender acquaintance with the world must convince every man that actions, not words, are the true criterion of the attachment of friends; and that the most liberal professions of good-will are very far from being the surest marks of it.

To contract new debts is not the way to pay old ones.

[Gaming] is the child of avarice, the brother of iniquity, and the father of mischief.

To persevere in one's duty and be silent, is the best answer to calumny.

When we assumed the soldier, we did not lay aside the citizen.

Laws made by common consent must not be trampled on by individuals.

Undertake not what you cannot perform, but be careful to keep your promise.

The tumultuous populace of large cities are ever to be dreaded.

Of all the animosities which have existed among

mankind, those which are caused by a difference of sentiments in religion appear to be the most inveterate and distressing, and ought most to be deprecated.

We ought not to look back unless it is to derive useful lessons from past errors, and for the purpose of profiting by dearly bought experience.

Associate yourself with men of good quality if you esteem your own reputation, for 'tis better to be alone than in bad company.

Be courteous to all but intimate with few, and let those few be well tried before you give them your confidence; true friendship is a plant of slow growth, and must undergo and withstand the shocks of adversity before it is entitled to the appellation.

[on taking the oath of office] I walk on untrodden ground. There is scarcely any part of my conduct that may not hereafter be drawn into precedent.

Liberty, when it begins to take root, is a plant of rapid growth.

As the sword was the last resort for the preservation of our liberties, so it ought to be the first to be laid aside when those liberties are firmly established.

There is nothing so likely to produce peace as to be well prepared to meet an enemy.

The most sincere neutrality is not a sufficient guard against the depredations of nations at war. To secure a respect to a neutral flag requires a naval force organized and ready to vindicate it from insult or aggression.

If, in the opinion of the people, the distribution or modification of the constitutional powers be in any particular wrong, let it be corrected by an amendment in the way which the Constitution designates. But let there be no change by usurpation.

As the first of everything, in our situation, will serve to establish a precedent, it is devoutly wished on my part, that these precedents may be fixed on true principles.

[on Washington's appointment as Commander in Chief] As to pay, Sir, I beg leave to assure the Congress that as no pecuniary consideration could have tempted me to accept this arduous employment at the expense of my domestic ease and happiness, I do not wish to make any profit from it.

My movements to the chair of government will be accompanied by feelings not unlike those of a culprit who is going to the place of his execution.

[on political parties] However [they] may now and then answer popular ends, they are likely in the course of time and things, to become potent engines, by which cunning, ambitious, and un-principled men will be enabled to subvert the power of the people and to usurp for themselves the reins of government, destroying afterwards the very engines which have lifted them to un-just dominion.

My ardent desire is, and my aim has been, to comply strictly with all our engagements, for-eign and domestic; but to keep the United States free from political connections with every other country, to see them independent of all and under the influence of none.

There can be no greater error than to expect, or calculate upon, real favors from nation to na-tion.

The nation which indulges toward another an habitual hatred or an habitual fondness is in some degree a slave. It is a slave to its animosity or to its affection, either of which is sufficient to lead it astray from its duty and its interest.

Patriotism . . . must be aided by a prospective in-terest or some reward. For a time, it may of it-self push men into action, to bear much, to encounter difficulties. But it will not endure unassisted by interest.

The aggregate happiness of society, which is best promoted by the practice of a virtuous policy, is, or ought to be, the end of all government.

Let us raise a standard to which the wise and honest can repair; the rest is in the hands of God.

The administration of justice is the firmest pillar of the government.

I never mean, unless some particular circumstances should compel me to do it, to possess another slave by purchase, it being among my first wishes to see some plan adopted by which slavery in this country may be abolished by law.

[last words] It is well, I die hard, but am not afraid to go.

John Adams
Born October 30, 1735—Died July 4, 1826
2nd President, 1797–1801 ★ Federalist

Ambition is the subtlest beast of the intellectual and moral field. It is wonderfully adroit in concealing itself from its owner.

Did you ever see a portrait of a great man without perceiving strong traits of pain and anxiety?

The jaws of power are always open to devour, and her arm is always stretched out, if possible, to destroy the freedom of thinking, speaking, and writing.

Power naturally grows. Why? Because human passions are insatiable.

It is weakness rather than wickedness which renders men unfit to be trusted with unlimited power.

Every project has been found no better than committing the lamb to the custody of the wolf, except that one which is called balance of power.

The executive powers lodged in the Senate are the most dangerous to the Constitution, and to liberty, of all the powers in it. The people then, ought to consider the President's office as the indispensable guardian of their rights.

[to Thomas Jefferson] You are apprehensive of monarchy; I, of aristocracy. I would therefore have given more power to the President and less to the Senate.

Rulers are no more than attorneys, agents, and trustees, for the people.

The essence of a free government consists in an effective control of rivalries.

In the first place, what is your definition of a republic? Mine is this: a government whose sovereignty is vested in more than one person.

The first of qualities for a great statesman is to be honest. And if it were possible that this opinion were an error, I should rather carry it with me to my grave than to believe that a man cannot be a statesman without being dishonest.

Be not intimidated . . . from publishing with the utmost freedom whatever can be warranted by the laws of your country; nor suffer yourselves to be wheedled out of your liberty by any pretenses of politeness, delicacy or decency. These, as they are often used, are but three different names for hypocrisy, chicanery and cowardice.

The numbers of men in all ages have preferred ease, slumber, and good cheer to liberty, when they have been in competition.

I would define liberty to be a power to do as we would be done by.

Liberty cannot be preserved without knowledge among people.

The preservation of the means of knowledge among the lowest ranks is of more importance than all the property of all the rich men in the country.

And after all that can be done to disseminate knowledge, you can never equalize it.

Liberty, according to my metaphysics, is a self-determining power in an intellectual agent. It implies thought, choice, and power.

Posterity! You will never know how much it cost the present generation to preserve your freedom! I hope you will make good use of it! If you do not, I shall repent it in Heaven that I ever took half the pains to preserve it!

If there is a form of government, then, whose principle and foundation is virtue, will not every sober man acknowledge it better calculated to promote the general happiness than any other form?

Public virtue cannot exist without private virtue.

The rich are seldom remarkable for modesty, ingenuity, or humanity. Their wealth has rather a tendency to make them penurious and selfish.

As the happiness of the people is the sole end of government, so the consent of the people is the only foundation of it.

[on the Boston Tea Party] The people should never rise without doing something to be remembered, something notable and striking. This destruction of the tea is so bold, so daring, so firm, intrepid, and inflexible, and it must have [such] important consequences, and so lasting, that I cannot but consider it as an epoch in history.

Let me have my farm, family and goose quill, and all the honors and offices this world has to bestow may go to those who deserve them better and desire them more. I court them not.

I must study politics and war that my sons may have liberty to study mathematics and philosophy.

The die was now cast; I had passed the Rubicon. Swim or sink, live or die, survive or perish with my country was my unalterable determination.

[on the vice-presidency] My country has, in its wisdom, contrived for me the most insignificant office that ever the invention of man contrived or his imagination conceived.

No man who ever held the office of President would congratulate a friend on obtaining it. He will make one man ungrateful, and a hundred men his enemies, for every office he can bestow.

Being the President was the four most miserable years of my life.

When I was young, and addicted to reading, I had heard about dancing on the points of metaphysical needles; but, by mixing in the world, I found the points of political needles finer and sharper than the metaphysical ones.

You will never be alone with a poet in your pocket.

Thomas Jefferson
Born April 13, 1743—Died July 4, 1826
3rd President, 1801–1809
★ *Democratic-Republican*

[on the presidency] To myself, personally, it brings nothing but unceasing drudgery and daily loss of friends.

The second office of the government is honorable and easy; the first is but a splendid misery.

If I could not go to heaven but with a party, I would not go there at all.

Whenever a man has cast a longing eye on offices, a rottenness begins in his conduct.

When a man assumes a public trust, he should consider himself as public property.

[Great Britain is] a pirate spreading misery and ruin over the face of the ocean.

Resistance to tyrants is obedience to God.

Question with boldness even the existence of God; because, if there be one, he must more approve of the homage of reason than that of blindfolded fear.

Establish the eternal truth that acquiescence under insult is not the way to escape war.

Experience has already shown that the impeachment the Constitution has provided is not even a scarecrow.

If congressmen talk too much, how can it be otherwise in a body to which the people send one hundred and fifty lawyers, whose trade it is to question everything, yield nothing, and talk by the hour.

In matters of principle, stand like a rock; in matters of taste, swim with the current.

It does me no injury for my neighbor to say there are twenty gods or no God. It neither picks my pocket nor breaks my leg.

It behooves every man who values liberty of conscience for himself, to resist invasions of it in the case of others.

Ignorance of the law is not an excuse in any country. If it were, the laws would lose their effect, because it can always be pretended.

I believe that justice is instinct and innate, that the moral sense is as much a part of our constitution as that of feeling, seeing, or hearing.

No man has a natural right to commit aggression on the equal rights of another; and this is all from which the laws ought to restrain him.

Laws are made for men of ordinary understanding, and should therefore be construed by the ordinary rules of common sense. Their meaning is not to be sought for in metaphysical subtleties, which may make anything mean everything or nothing, at pleasure.

I like the dreams of the future better than the history of the past.

I'm a great believer in luck, and I find the harder I work the more I have of it.

Science is my passion, politics my duty.

I think it is Montaigne who has said, that ignorance is the softest pillow on which a man can rest his head. I am sure it is true as to everything political, and shall endeavor to estrange myself to everything of that character.

We can no longer say there is nothing new under the sun. For this whole chapter in the history of man is new.

A bill of rights is what the people are entitled to against every government on earth, general or particular; and what no just government should refuse, or rest on inference.

We hold these truths to be self-evident,—that all

men are created equal; that they are endowed by their creator with certain inalienable rights; that among these are life, liberty, and the pursuit of happiness.

All eyes are opened or opening to the rights of man. . . . The mass of mankind has not been born with saddles on their backs, nor a favored few booted and spurred, ready to ride them legitimately, by the grace of God.

The ball of liberty is not so well in motion that it will roll round the globe.

Timid men prefer the calm of despotism to the boisterous sea of liberty.

The time to guard against corruption and tyranny is before they shall have gotten hold of us. It is better to keep the wolf out of the fold than to trust to drawing his teeth and talons after he shall have entered.

The tree of liberty must be refreshed from time to time with the blood of patriots and tyrants. It is its natural manure.

We are not to expect to be translated from despotism to liberty in a feather bed.

If a state expects to be ignorant and free, in a state of civilization, it expects what never was and never will be.

I know of no safe depository of the ultimate powers of society but the people themselves; and if we think them not enlightened enough to exercise their control with a wholesome discretion, the remedy is not to take it from them, but to inform their discretion by education.

[Education] engrafts a new man on the native stock, and improves what in his nature was vicious and perverse into qualities of virtue and social worth.

History, in general, only informs us what bad government is.

The natural progress of things is for liberty to yield and government to gain ground.

That government is best which governs the least, because its people discipline themselves.

It is error alone which needs the support of government. Truth can stand by itself.

It is not by the consolidation, or concentration, of powers, but by their distribution that good government is effected.

If a due participation of office is a matter of right, how are vacancies to be obtained? Those by death are few; by resignation none. *[commonly paraphrased as "Few die and none resign"]*

I sincerely believe that banking establishments

are more dangerous than standing armies, and that the principle of spending money to be paid by posterity, under the name of funding, is but swindling futurity on a large scale.

Equal and exact justice to all men, of whatever state or persuasion, religious or political; peace, commerce and honest friendship with all nations—entangling alliances with none.

Nothing can now be believed which is seen in a newspaper. Truth itself becomes suspicious by being put into that polluted vehicle.

Defamation is becoming a necessity of life; inasmuch as a dish of tea in the morning or evening cannot be digested without that stimulant.

The man who fears no truth has nothing to fear from a lie.

The man who never looks into a newspaper is better informed than he who reads them; inasmuch as he who knows nothing is nearer the truth than he whose mind is filled with falsehoods and errors.

Our liberty depends upon freedom of the press, and that cannot be limited without being lost.

Error of opinion may be tolerated where reason is left free to combat it.

Were it left to me to decide whether we should

have a government without newspapers, or newspapers without a government, I should not hesitate a moment to prefer the latter.

To the press alone, chequered as it is with abuses, the world is indebted for all the triumphs which have been gained by reason and humanity over error and oppression.

The opinions of men are not the object of civil government, nor under its jurisdiction.

Amplification is the vice of the modern orator. Speeches measured by the hour die by the hour.

The most valuable of all talents is that of never using two words when one will do.

Never spend your money before you have it.

Never buy what you do not want, because it is cheap; it will be dear to you.

Whenever you are to do a thing, though it can never be known but to yourself, ask yourself how you would act were all the world looking at you, and act accordingly.

No person will have occasion to complain of the want of time who never loses any.

I have not observed men's honesty to increase with their riches.

He who permits himself to tell a lie once finds it

much easier to do it a second and a third time till at length it becomes habitual.

Victory and defeat are each of the same price.

It is in our lives and not from our words, that our religion must be read.

Life is the art of avoiding pain.

Of all the cankers of human happiness, none corrodes it with so silent, yet so baneful a tooth, as indolence.

The bulk of mankind are schoolboys through life.

Men are disposed to live honestly, if the means of doing so are open to them.

It is neither wealth nor splendor, but tranquility and occupation, which give happiness.

An injured friend is the bitterest of foes.

Take things always by their smooth handle.

Do not bite at the bait of pleasure till you know there is no hook beneath it.

Were we to love none who had imperfections, this would be a desert for our love.

Delay is preferable to error.

We never repent of having eaten too little.

How much pain have cost us the evils which have never happened.

I find the pain of a little censure, even when it is unfounded, is more acute than the pleasure of much praise.

He is happiest of whom the world says least, good or bad.

James Madison
Born March 16, 1751—Died June 28, 1836
4th President, 1809–1817
★ *Democratic-Republican*

[*on the Constitution*] Every word decides a question between power and liberty.

But what is government itself, but the greatest of all reflections on human nature? If men were angels, no government would be necessary.

The essence of government is power; and power, lodged in human hands, will ever be liable to abuse.

It is a melancholy reflection that liberty should be equally exposed to danger whether the government have too much or too little power.

What is the meaning of government? An institution to make people do their duty. A government leaving it to a man to do his duty, or not, as he pleases, would be a new species of government, or rather no government at all.

Justice is the end of government. It is the end of civil society. It ever has been and ever will be pursued until it be obtained, or until liberty be lost in the pursuit.

There is nothing stable but heaven and the Constitution.

Liberty may be endangered by the abuses of liberty as well as the abuses of power.

The nation which reposes on the pillow of political confidence, will sooner or later end its political existence in a deadly lethargy.

Since the general civilization of mankind, I believe there are more instances of the abridgement of the freedom of the people, by gradual and silent encroachments of those in power, than by violent and sudden usurpations.

Temporary deviations from fundamental principles are always more or less dangerous. When the first pretext fails, those who become interested in prolonging the evil will rarely be at a loss for other pretexts.

Perhaps it is a universal truth that the loss of liberty at home is to be charged to provisions against danger, real or pretended, from abroad.

The most common and durable source of factions has been the various and unequal distribution of property.

Those who hold and those who are without

property have ever formed distinct interests in society. Those who are creditors, and those who are debtors, fall under a like discrimination.

Our forefathers brought the germ of independence in the principle of self-taxation.

I go on the principle that a public debt is a public curse.

Could it be so arranged that every newspaper, when printed on one side should be handed over to the press of an adversary, to be printed on the other, thus presenting to every reader both sides of every question, truth would always have a fair chance. But such a remedy is ideal.

Religious bondage shackles and debilitates the mind, and unfits it for every noble enterprise.

A certain degree of misery seems inseparable from a high degree of populousness.

A certain degree of preparation for war is not only indispensable to avert disasters in the onset, but affords also the best security for the continuance of peace.

Learned institutions ought to be favorite objects with every free people. They throw that light over the public mind which is the best security against crafty and dangerous encroachments on the public liberty.

A popular government, without popular information, or the means of acquiring it, is but a prologue to a farce or a tragedy; or, perhaps both. Knowledge will forever govern ignorance; and a people who mean to be their own governors, must arm themselves with the power which knowledge gives.

The diffusion of knowledge is the only guardian of true liberty.

The capacity of the female mind for studies of the highest order cannot be doubted, having been sufficiently illustrated by its works of genius, of erudition, and of science.

Having outlived so many of my contemporaries, I ought not to forget that I may be thought to have outlived myself.

Conscience is the most sacred of all property.

James Monroe
Born April 28, 1758—Died July 4, 1831
5th President, 1817–1825
★ *Democratic-Republican*

The right of self-defense never ceases. It is among the most sacred, and alike necessary to nations and to individuals.

Preparation for war is a constant stimulus to suspicion and ill-will.

The history of all ages proves that . . . at least one half of every century, in ancient as well as modern times, has been consumed in wars, and often of the most general and desolating character.

A complete remedy to a political disease is seldom found until something like a crisis occurs, and this is promoted by the abuse of those who have rendered the most important services, and whose characters will bear the test of enquiry.

The revolution of France undoubtedly took its origin from that of the United States. Her citizens fought and bled within our service. They caught the spirit of liberty here, and carried it home with them.

In this great nation there is but one order, that of the people.

Let us, by all wise and constitutional measures, promote intelligence among the people, as the best means of preserving our liberties.

In a government founded on the sovereignty of the people, the education of youth is an object of the first importance.

The best form of government is that which is most likely to prevent the greatest sum of evil.

Mrs. Monroe hath added a daughter to our society who though noisy, contributes greatly to its amusement.

A little flattery will support a man through great fatigue.

The circulation of confidence is better than the circulation of money.

It is possible I may lose my scalp from the temper of the Indians, but if either a little fighting or a great deal of running will save it, I shall escape safe.

To remove [Native Americans] from . . . the territory on which they now reside, by force, even with a view to their own security and happiness would be revolting to humanity and utterly unjustifiable. Between the limits of our present states and territories and the Rocky Mountains and Mexico there is a vast territory, to which they might be invited with inducements which might be successful.

[Monroe Doctrine] The American continents . . . are henceforth not to be considered as subjects for future colonization by any European powers.

So seducing is the passion for extending our territory, that if compelled to take our own redress it is quite uncertain within what limit it will be confined.

John Quincy Adams
Born July 11, 1767—Died February 23, 1848
6th President, 1825–1829
★ *Democratic-Republican*

To believe all men honest would be folly. To believe none so is something worse.

Our Constitution professedly rests upon the good sense and attachment of the people. This basis, weak as it may appear, has not yet been found to fail.

Always vote for a principle, though you vote alone, and you may cherish the sweet reflection that your vote is never lost.

I am a man of reserved, cold, austere, and forbidding manners; my political adversaries say, a gloomy misanthropist, and my personal enemies, an unsocial savage. With a knowledge of the actual defect in my character, I have not the pliability to reform it.

I had much rather you should impute to me great error of judgment than the smallest deviation from sincerity.

I would take not one step to advance or promote pretensions to the presidency. If that office was to be the prize of cabal and intrigue, of purchasing newspapers, bribing by appointments, or bargaining for foreign missions, I had no ticket in that lottery.

A public life ought to be a perpetual sacrifice of resentments.

There is nothing so deep and nothing so shallow which political enmity will not turn to account.

In the turbid stream of political life, a conscientious man must endeavor to do justice to all, and to return good for evil, but he must always expect evil in return.

[on the presidency] I can scarcely conceive a more harassing, wearying, teasing condition of existence. It literally renders life burdensome. What retirement will be I cannot realize, but have formed no favorable anticipation. It cannot be worse than this perpetual motion and crazing cares.

[on Thomas Jefferson] His genius is of the old French school. It conceives better than it combines.

Law logic—an artificial system of reasoning, exclusively used in the courts of justice, but good for nothing anywhere else.

The soul of one man cannot by human law be made the property of another. The owner of a slave is the owner of a living corpse; but he is not the owner of the man.

By the laws of nature and nature's God, man cannot be the property of man.

Slavery is the great and foul stain upon the North American union, and it is a contemplation worthy of the most exalted whether its total abolition is or is not practicable.

That nature's God commands the slave to rise
And on the oppressor's head to break his chain.
Roll, years of promise, rapidly roll round,
Till not a slave shall on this earth be found.

I consider an unjust war as the greatest of all human atrocities, but I esteem a just one as the highest of all human virtues.

[on the Monroe Doctrine] American continents are no longer subjects for European colonial establishments.

The most healing of medicines, unduly administered, becomes the most deadly of poisons.

Among the first, perhaps the very first, instrument for the improvement of the condition of men is knowledge.

My wants are many, and, if told,
Would muster many a score;
And were each wish a mint of gold,
I still should long for more.

I can never be sure of writing a line that will not some day be published by friend or foe. Nor can I write a sentence susceptible of an odious misconstruction but it will be seized upon and bandied about like a watchword for hatred and derision. This condition of things gives style the cramp.

Literature has been the charm of my life, and, could I have carved out my own fortunes, to literature would my whole life have been devoted.

[last words] This is the last of earth! I am content.

Andrew Jackson
Born March 15, 1767—Died June 8, 1845
7th President, 1829–1837 ★ Democrat

One man with courage makes a majority.

In a free government the demand for moral qualities should be made superior to that of talents.

Perpetuity is stamped upon the Constitution by the blood of our fathers.

Each public officer who takes an oath to support the Constitution swears that he will support it as he understands, and not as it is understood by others.

Mere precedent is a dangerous source of authority.

The wisdom of man never yet contrived a system of taxation that would operate with perfect equality.

The murderer only takes the life of the parent and leaves his character as a goodly heritage to his children, whilst the slanderer takes away his goodly reputation and leaves him a living monument to his children's disgrace.

I know what I am fit for. I can command a body of men in a rough way; but I am not fit to be President.

[on the presidency] I can with truth say mine is a situation of dignified slavery.

[and]

Private life would be a paradise compared to the best situation here; and if once more there, it would take a writ of habeas corpus to remove me into public life again.

We have all read history, and is it not certain, that of all aristocracies mere wealth is the most odious, rapacious, and tyrannical?

The moment a person forms a theory, his imagination sees in every object only the traits that favor that theory.

In general, the great can protect themselves, but the poor and humble, require the arm and shield of the law.

The brave man inattentive to his duty, is worth little more to his country than the coward who deserts her in the hour of danger.

All bigotries hang to one another.

[on Sam Houston] A man made by God and not by a tailor.

Temporize not! It is always injurious.

There are, perhaps, few men who can for any length of time enjoy office and power without being more or less under the influence of feelings unfavorable to the faithful discharge of their political duties.

If such corruption exists in the green tree, what will be in the dry?

There are no necessary evils in government. Its evils exist only in its abuses. If it would confine itself to equal protection, and, as Heaven does its rains, shower its favors alike on the high and the low, the rich and the poor, it would be an unqualified blessing.

Heaven will be no heaven to me if I do not meet my wife there.

Martin Van Buren

Born December 5, 1782—Died July 24, 1862
8th President, 1837–1841 ★ Democrat

Is it possible to be anything in this country without being a politician?

Most men are not scolded out of their opinion.

Indebtedness cannot be lessened by borrowing more money, or by changing the form of the debt.

Wealth can only be accumulated by the earnings of industry and the savings of frugality.

[on slavery] No evil can result from its inhibition more pernicious than its toleration.

There is a power in public opinion in this country—and I thank God for it: for it is the most honest and best of all powers—which will not tolerate an incompetent or unworthy man to hold in his weak or wicked hands the lives and fortunes of his fellow-citizens.

In the shock of contending empires it is only by assuming a resolute bearing and clothing themselves with defensive armor that neutral nations can maintain their independent rights.

The framers of our excellent Constitution and the people who approved it . . . wisely judged that the less government interferes with private pursuits the better for the general prosperity.

As to the presidency, the two happiest days of my life were those of my entry upon the office and of my surrender of it.

William Henry Harrison
Born February 9, 1773—Died April 4, 1841
9th President, 1841 (served one month) ★ *Whig*

Power is insinuating. Few men are satisfied with less power than they are able to procure. No lover is ever satisfied with the first smile of his mistress.

There is nothing more corrupting, nothing more destructive of the noblest and finest feelings of our nature, than the exercise of unlimited power.

We admit of no government by divine right, believing that so far as power is concerned the beneficent creator has made no distinction amongst men.

I contend that the strongest of all governments is that which is most free.

Conscience is that magistrate of God in the human heart whose still small voice the loudest revelry cannot drown.

The plea of necessity, that eternal argument of all conspirators.

A decent and manly examination of the acts of government should be not only tolerated, but encouraged.

If political parties in a republic are necessary to secure a degree of vigilance to keep the public functionaries within bounds of law and duty, at that point their usefulness ends.

[about himself] Some folks are silly enough to have formed a plan to make a President of the United States out of this clerk and clodhopper.

John Tyler
Born March 29, 1790—Died January 18, 1862
10th President, 1841–1845 ★ Whig

[campaign slogan] Tippecanoe and Tyler, Too.

Popularity, I have always thought, may aptly be compared to a coquette—the more you woo her, the more apt is she to elude your embrace.

Patronage is the sword and cannon by which war may be made on the liberty of the human race. . . . Give the President control over the purse—the power to place the immense revenues of the country into any hands he may please, and I care not what you call him, he is "every inch a king."

The Constitution never designed that the executive should be a mere cipher. On the contrary, it denies to Congress the right to pass any law without his approval.

The barking of newspapers and the brawling of demagogues can never drive me from my course.

If the tide of defamation and abuse shall turn, and my administration come to be praised, future Vice Presidents who may succeed to the presidency may feel some slight encouragement to pursue an independent course.

[inscription on the grave of his horse] Here lies the body of my good horse, "The General." For twenty years he bore me around the circuit of my practice, and in all that time he never made a blunder. Would that his master could say the same!

James Knox Polk
Born November 2, 1795—Died June 15, 1849
11th President, 1845–1849 ★ Democrat

We have a country as well as a party to obey.

Ours is not a consolidated empire, but a confederated union.

The President's power is negative merely, and not affirmative.

No President who performs his duties faithfully and conscientiously can have any leisure.

When it comes down to the relations of any President with a Congress controlled by the opposite party, I just say this: it is no bed of roses.

The passion for office among members of Congress is very great, if not absolutely disreputable, and greatly embarrasses the operations of the government. They create offices by their own votes and then seek to fill them themselves.

The people of the United States have no idea of the extent to which the President's time, which ought to be devoted to more important matters, is occupied by the voracious and often unprincipled persons who seek office.

One great object of the Constitution in conferring upon the President a qualified negative upon the legislation of Congress was to protect minorities from injustice and oppression by majorities.

In truth, though I occupy a very high position, I am the hardest-working man in this country.

I would keep as much money in the treasury as the safety of the government required, and no more. I would keep no surplus revenue there to scramble for, either for internal improvements, or for anything else. I would bring the government back to what it was intended to be—a plain economical government.

Public opinion: May it always perform one of its appropriate offices; by teaching the public functionaries of the state and federal government that neither shall assume the exercise of powers entrusted by the Constitution to the other.

I prefer to supervise the whole operations of the government myself rather than entrust the public business to subordinates and this makes my duties very great.

I am heartily rejoiced that my term is so near its close. I will soon cease to be a servant and will become a sovereign.

Zachary Taylor
Born November 24, 1784—Died July 9, 1850
12th President, 1849–1850 ★ Whig

If I occupy the White House, I must be untrammelled and unpledged, so as to be President of the nation and not of a party.

I will not make myself unhappy at what I cannot prevent, nor give up the Constitution or abandon it because a rent has been made in it, but will stick by and repair it, and nurse it as long as it will hang together.

Rotation in office, provided good men are appointed, is sound republican doctrine.

The axe, pick, saw and trowel, has become more the implement of the American soldier than the cannon, musket or sword.

It would be judicious to act with magnanimity towards a prostrate foe.

For more than half a century, during which kingdoms and empires have fallen, this Union has stood unshaken. The patriots who formed it have long since descended to the grave; yet still it remains, the proudest monument to their memory.

[on the presidency] I do not care a fig about the office.

Millard Fillmore
Born January 7, 1800—Died March 8, 1874
13th President, 1850–1853 ★ Whig

It is better to wear out than rust out.

Wars will occur until man changes his nature.

An honorable defeat is better than a dishonorable victory.

The man who can look upon a crisis without being willing to offer himself upon the altar of his country is not fit for public trust.

Church and state should be separate, not only in form, but fact—religion and politics should not be mingled.

The law is the only sure protection of the weak, and the only efficient restraint upon the strong.

Without law there can be no real practical liberty, that when the law is trampled under foot tyranny rules, whether it appears in the form of a military despotism or of popular violence.

Let us remember that revolutions do not always establish freedom. Our own free institutions were not the offspring of our revolution. They existed before.

God knows that I detest slavery, but it is an existing evil, for which we are not responsible, and we must endure it and give it such protection as is guaranteed by the Constitution, till we can get rid of it without destroying the last hope of free government in the world.

Three years of civil war have desolated the fairest portion of our land, loaded the country with an enormous debt that the sweat of millions yet unborn must be taxed to pay; arrayed brother against brother, father against son in mortal combat; deluged our country with fraternal blood, whitened our battle-fields with the bones of the slain, and darkened the sky with the pall of mourning.

[on declining an honorary degree from Oxford University] I had not the advantage of a classical education, and no man should, in my judgement, accept a degree he cannot read.

It is a national disgrace that our Presidents, after having occupied the highest position in the country, should be cast adrift, and, perhaps, be compelled to keep a corner grocery for subsistence.

Franklin Pierce
Born November 23, 1804—Died October 8, 1869
14th President, 1853–1857 ★ *Democrat*

[on Congress] In a body where there are more than one hundred talking lawyers . . . you can make no calculation upon the termination of any debate and frequently, the more trifling the subject, the more animated and protracted the discussion.

[campaign slogan] We Polked you in '44, We Shall Pierce you in '52.

If a man who has atttained this high office cannot free himself from cliques and act independently, our constitution is valueless.

I find that remark, "'Tis distance lends enchantment to the view" is no less true of the political than of the natural world.

I acknowledge my obligations to the masses of my countrymen, and to them alone.

The storm of frenzy and faction must inevitably dash itself in vain against the unshaken rock of the Constitution.

The revenue of the country, levied almost insensibly to the taxpayer, goes on from year to year, increasing beyond either the interests or the prospective wants of the government.

A republic without parties is a complete anomaly. The history of all popular governments shows how absurd is the idea of their attempting to exist without parties.

The stars upon your banner have become nearly threefold their original number; your densely populated possessions skirt the shores of the two great oceans.

James Buchanan
Born April 23, 1791—Died June 1, 1868
15th President, 1857–1861 ★ Democrat

The ballot box is the surest arbiter of disputes among free men.

Rest assured, that our population requires the curb more than the rein.

The march of free government on this continent must not be trammelled by the intrigues and selfish interests of European powers. Liberty must be allowed to work out its natural results; and these will, ere long, astonish the world.

There is nothing as stable but heaven and the constitution.

Abstract propositions should never be discussed by a legislative body.

Let us look the danger fairly in the face. Secession is neither more nor less than revolution.

What, sir! prevent the American people from crossing the Rocky Mountains? You might as well command Niagara not to flow. We must fulfill our destiny.

Self-preservation is the first instinct of nature, and therefore any state of society in which the sword is all the time suspended over the heads of the people must at last become intolerable.

Beware of elevating to the highest civil trust the commander of your victorious armies.

The distribution of patronage of the government is by far the most disagreeable duty of the President. Applicants are so numerous, and their applications are pressed with such eagerness by their friends both in and out of

Congress, that the selection of one for any desirable office gives offense to many.

My principles are convictions.

What is right and what is practicable are two different things.

A long visit to a friend is often a great bore. Never make people twice glad.

All the friends I loved and wanted to reward are dead and all the enemies I hated and had marked for punishment are turned my friends.

I acknowledge no master but the law.

[to Abraham Lincoln] If you are as happy, my dear sir, on entering [the White House] as I am in leaving it, you are the happiest man in the country!

Abraham Lincoln
Born February 12, 1809—Died April 15, 1865
16th President, 1861–1865 ★ Republican

A woman is the only thing I am afraid of that I know will not hurt me.

Whatever you are, be a good one.

The best thing about the future is that it comes only one day at a time.

Character is like a tree and reputation like its

shadow. The shadow is what we think of it; the tree is the real thing.

A fellow once came to me to ask for an appointment as a minister abroad. Finding he could not get that, he came down to some more modest position. Finally, he asked to be made a tide-waiter [i.e., a customs inspector]. When he saw he could not get that, he asked me for an old pair of trousers. It is sometimes well to be humble.

When you have got an elephant by the hind leg, and he is trying to run away, it's best to let him run.

I hold that if the Almighty had ever made a set of men that should do all the eating and none of the work, He would have made them with mouths only and no hands; and if He had ever made another class that He intended should do all the work and no eating, He would have made them with hands only and no mouths.

The Lord prefers common-looking people. That is the reason He makes so many of them.

Nobody has ever expected me to be President. In my poor lean, lank face, nobody has ever seen that any cabbages were sprouting out.

As a general rule, I abstain from reading the reports of attacks upon myself, wishing not to be provoked by that to which I cannot properly offer an answer.

[on the presidency] You have heard the story . . . about the man who was tarred and feathered and carried out of town on a rail? A man in the crowd asked him how he liked it. His reply was that if it was not for the honor of the thing, he would much rather walk.

I have been told I was on the road to hell, but I had no idea it was just a mile down the road with a dome on it.

To sin by silence when they should protest makes cowards of men.

In times like the present, men should utter nothing for which they would not willingly be responsible through time and in eternity.

The dogmas of the quiet past are inadequate to the stormy present. The occasion is piled high with difficulty; and we must rise with the occasion. As our case is new, so we must think anew and act anew. We must disenthrall ourselves.

Towering genius disdains a beaten path. It seeks regions hitherto unexplored.

With public sentiment, nothing can fail; without it, nothing can succeed.

"A house divided against itself cannot stand." I

believe this government cannot endure permanently half-slave and half-free. I do not expect the Union to be dissolved—I do not expect the house to fall—but I do expect it will cease to be divided. It will become all one thing, or all the other.

We must settle this question now—whether in a free government the minority have the right to break it up whenever they choose. If we fail, it will go far to prove the incapability of the people to govern themselves.

The central idea of secession is the essence of anarchy.

When the hour comes for dealing with slavery, I trust I will be willing to do my duty though it cost my life.

If slavery is not wrong, nothing is wrong.

[on meeting Harriet Beecher Stowe] So you're the little woman who wrote the book that made this great war!

Whenever I hear anyone arguing for slavery, I feel a strong impulse to see it tried on him personally.

As I would not be a slave, so I would not be a master. This expresses my idea of democracy.

In giving freedom to the slave we assure freedom

to the free,—honorable alike in what we give and what we preserve.

I hate [slavery] because it deprives the republican example of its just influence in the world—enables the enemies of free institutions, with plausibility, to taunt us as hypocrites—causes the real friends of freedom to doubt our sincerity.

Such will be a great lesson of peace: teaching men that what they cannot take by an election, neither can they take it by war.

It has been said of the world's history hitherto that might makes right. It is for us and for our time to reverse the maxim, and to say that right makes might.

He who does something at the head of one regiment will eclipse him who does nothing at the head of a hundred.

I wish some of you would tell me the brand of whiskey that Grant drinks. I would like to send a barrel of it to my other generals.

Military glory—that attractive rainbow that rises in showers of blood, that serpent's eye that charms to destroy.

We shall sooner have the bird by hatching the egg than by smashing it.

I have always found that mercy bears richer fruits than strict justice.

It has been my experience that folks who have no vices have very few virtues.

Tact is the ability to describe others as they see themselves.

Truth is generally the best vindication against slander.

My best friend is the man who'll get me a book I ain't read.

Human action can be modified to some extent, but human nature cannot be changed.

If both factions, or neither, shall abuse you, you will probably be about right. Beware of being assailed by one, and praised by the other.

We better know there is a fire whence we see much smoke rising than we could know it by one or two witnesses swearing to it. The witnesses may commit perjury, but the smoke cannot.

What is conservatism? Is it not adherence to the old and tried, against the new and untried?

The shepherd drives the wolf from the sheep's throat, for which the sheep thanks the shepherd as his liberator, while the wolf denounces him for the same act. . . . Plainly the sheep and the wolf are not agreed upon a definition of liberty.

Prohibition will work great injury to the cause of temperance. It is a species of intemperance within itself, for it goes beyond the bounds of reason in that it attempts to control a man's appetite by legislation, and makes a crime out of things that are not crimes.

[on a fellow lawyer] He can compress the most words into the smallest ideas of any man I ever met.

Discourage litigation. Persuade your neighbors to compromise whenever you can. . . . As a peacemaker the lawyer has a superior opportunity of being a good man. There will still be business enough.

I desire to see the time when education, and by its means, morality, sobriety, enterprise and industry, shall become much more general than at present.

I claim not to have controlled events, but confess plainly that events have controlled me.

Yield larger things to which you can show no more than equal right; and yield lesser ones, though clearly your own. Better give your path to a dog than be bitten by him in contesting for the right. Even killing the dog would not cure the bite.

If you once forfeit the confidence of your fellow citizens, you can never regain their respect and esteem. It is true that you may fool all the people some of the time; you can even fool some of the people all the time; but you can't fool all of the people all the time.

We are not enemies, but friends. . . . Though passion may have strained, it must not break our bonds of affection. The mystic chords of memory, stretching from every battlefield, and patriot grave, to every living heart and hearth-stone all over this broad land, will yet swell the chorus of the Union, when again touched, as surely they will be, by the better angels of our nature.

We shall nobly save, or meanly lose, the last best hope of earth.

Four score and seven years ago our fathers brought forth on this continent, a new nation, conceived in liberty, and dedicated to the proposition that all men are created equal. . . . [F]rom these honored dead we take increased devotion to that cause for which they gave the last full measure of devotion—that we here highly re-solve that these dead shall not have died in vain—that this nation, under God, shall have a new birth of freedom—and that government of the people, by the people, for the people, shall not perish from the earth.

With malice toward none; with charity for all; with firmness in the right, as God gives us to see the right, let us strive on to finish the work we are in: to bind up the nation's wounds.

If I am killed, I can die but once; but to live in constant dread of it, is to die over and over again.

Andrew Johnson
Born December 29, 1808—Died July 31, 1875
17th President, 1865–1869 ★ Democrat

Secession is hell-born and hell-bound.

There are no good laws but such as repeal other laws.

Honest conviction is my courage, the Constitution is my guide.

The goal to strive for is a poor government but a rich people.

In the support and practice of correct principles we can never reach wrong results.

Away with slavery, the breeder of aristocrats. Up with the Stars and Stripes, symbol of free labor and free men.

If the rabble were lopped off at one end and the aristocrat at the other, all would be well with the country.

A railroad! It would frighten horses, put the owners of public vehicles out of business, break up inns and taverns, and be a monopoly generally.

Notwithstanding a mendacious press, notwithstanding a subsidized gang of hirelings who have not ceased to traduce me, I have discharged all my official duties and fulfilled my pledges. And I say here tonight that if my predecessor had lived, the vials of wrath would have poured out upon him.

When I die, I desire no better winding sheet than the Stars and Stripes, and no softer pillow than the Constitution of my country.

Ulysses Simpson Grant
Born April 27, 1822—Died July 23, 1885
18th President, 1869–1877 ★ Republican

God gave us Lincoln and Liberty, let us fight for both.

[on the surrender of General Robert E. Lee at Appomattox] I felt like anything rather than rejoicing at the downfall of a foe who had fought so long and so valiantly.

The effects of the late civil war have been to free the slave and make him a citizen. Yet he is not possessed of the civil rights which citizenship should carry with it. This is wrong and should be corrected.

Treat the Negro as a citizen and a voter, as he is and must remain, and soon parties will be divided not on the color line but on principle.

The art of war is simple enough. Find out where your enemy is. Get at him as soon as you can. Strike him as hard as you can, and keep moving.

Wars produce many stories of fiction, some of which are told until they are believed to be true.

There never was a time when, in my opinion, some way could not be found to prevent the drawing of the sword.

To maintain peace in the future it is necessary to be prepared for war.

I am more of a farmer than a soldier. I take little or no interest in military affairs.

I shall on all subjects have a policy to recommend, but none to enforce against the will of the people.

I know no method to secure the repeal of bad or obnoxious laws so effective as their stringent execution.

Whatever there is of greatness in the United States is due to labor. The laborer is the author of all greatness and wealth. Without labor there would be no government and no leading class.

Keep the church and the state forever separate.

I would suggest the taxation of all property equally whether church or corporation.

The theory of government changes with general progress.

My failures have been errors of judgment, not of intent.

I believe that our Great Maker is preparing the world in His own good time to become one nation, speaking one language, when armies and navies will no longer be required.

I know only two tunes; one of them is "Yankee Doodle," and the other isn't.

Rutherford Birchard Hayes
Born October 4, 1822—Died January 17, 1893
19th President, 1877–1881 ★ Republican

"Practical politics" means selfish ends promoted by base means.

The melancholy thing in our public life is the insane desire to get higher.

He serves his party best who serves his country best.

I would honor the man who would give to his country a good newspaper.

The practice of annexing general legislation to apropriation has become a serious abuse. Every measure should stand on its own bottom.

Fighting battles is like courting girls: those who make the most pretensions and are boldest usually win.

As knowledge spreads, wealth spreads. To diffuse knowledge is to diffuse wealth. To give all an equal chance to acquire knowledge is the best and surest way to give all an equal chance to acquire property.

[on war] People forget self. . . . People are more generous, more sympathetic, better, than when engaged in the more selfish pursuits of peace.

All appointments *hurt.* Five friends are made cold or hostile for every appointment; no *new* friends are made. All patronage is perilous to men of real ability or merit. It aids only those who lack other claims to public support.

It is now true that this is God's country, if equal rights—a fair start and an equal chance in the race of life —are everywhere secured to all.

I am not liked as a President by the politicians in office, in the press, or in Congress. But I am content to abide the judgment—the sober second thought—of the people.

[on the presidency] Well I am heartily tired of this life of bondage, responsibility and toil.

James Abram Garfield
Born November 19, 1831—Died September 19, 1881
20th President, 1881 (served six months)
★ *Republican*

I would rather believe something and suffer for it, than to slide along into success without opinions.

I love agitation and investigation and glory in defending unpopular truth against popular error.

Things don't turn up in this world until somebody turns them up.

An Englishman who was wrecked on a strange shore and wandering along the coast came to a gallows with a victim hanging on it, and fell down on his knees and thanked God that he at last beheld a sign of civilization.

Tonight I am a private citizen. Tomorrow, I shall be called to assume new responsibilities and, on the day after, the broadside of the world's wrath will strike.

[on the presidency] My God! What is there in this place that a man should ever want to get into it?

It had better be known in the outset whether the President is the head of the government, or the registering clerk of the Senate.

If you are not too large for the place you now occupy, you are too small for it.

I am casting about me to find someone who will help to enliven the solitude which surrounds the presidency. The unfortunate incumbent of that office is the most isolated man in America.

Talleyrand once said to the first Napoleon that "the United States is a giant without bones." Since that time our gristle has been rapidly hardening.

I found a kind of party terrorism pervading and oppressing the minds of our best men.

All free governments are party governments.

I have so long and so often seen the evil effects of the presidential fever upon my associates and friends that I am determined it shall not seize upon me.

The possession of great powers no doubt carries with it a contempt for mere external show.

Real political issues cannot be manufactured by the leaders of political parties. The real political issues of the day declare themselves, and come out of the depths of that deep which we call public opinion.

Lincoln said in his homely way that he wanted "to take a bath in public opinion." I think I have a right to take a bath before I do much talking.

A law is not a law without coercion behind it.

It will cost me some struggle to keep from despising the office seeker.

[Office seekers] open their mouths for a horse, but are perfectly willing to settle for a fly.

A brave man is a man who dares to look the devil in the face and tell him he is a devil.

History is but the unrolled scroll of prophecy.

Justice and goodwill will outlast passion.

Take off the strong cord of discipline and morality, and you will be an old man before your twenties are past. Preserve these forces. Do not burn them out in idleness or crime.

A pound of pluck is worth a ton of luck.

The chief danger which threatens the influence and honor of the press is the tendency of its liberty to degenerate into license.

Congress lives in the blaze of "that fierce light which beats against the throne." The press and the telegraph will tomorrow morning announce at a million breakfast tables what has been said and done in Congress today.

It is alleged that in many communities Negro citizens are practically denied the freedom of the ballot. It is a crime which, if persisted in, will destroy the government itself.

All free governments are managed by the combined wisdom and folly of the people.

This nation must open up new avenues of work and usefulness to the women of this country.

Only radicals have accomplished anything in a great crisis.

Ideas are the great warriors of the world, and a war which has no ideas behind it, is simply a brutality.

Next in importance to freedom and justice is popular education, without which neither freedom nor justice can be permanently maintained.

Assassination can be no more guarded against than death by lightning; and it is best not to worry about either.

Chester Alan Arthur
Born October 5, 1830—Died November 18, 1886
21st President, 1881–1885 ★ Republican

I may be President of the United States, but my private life is nobody's damn business.

If it were not for the reporters, I would tell you the truth.

No higher or more assuring proof could exist of the strength and permanence of popular government than the fact that though the chosen of the people be struck down, his constitutional successor is peacefully installed without shock or strain except the sorrow which mourns the bereavement.

If we heed the teachings of history, we shall not forget that in the life of every nation emergencies may arise when a resort to arms can alone save it from dishonor.

Well, there doesn't seem to be anything else for an ex-President to do but go into the country and raise big pumpkins.

Grover Cleveland

Born March 18, 1837—Died June 24, 1908
22nd & 24th President, 1885–1889 & 1893–1897
★ *Democrat*

A man is known by the company he keeps, and also by the company from which he is kept out.

I am not concerning myself about what history will think, but contenting myself with the approval of this fellow named Cleveland whom I have generally found to be a pretty good sort of fellow.

He mocks the people who proposes that the government shall protect the rich and that they in turn will care for the laboring poor.

The truly American sentiment recognizes the dignity of labor and the fact that honor lies in honest toil.

Under our scheme of government the waste of public money is a crime against the citizen.

The lessons of paternalism ought to be unlearned and the better lesson taught that while the people should patriotically and cheerfully support their government, its functions do not include the support of the people.

Must we always look for the political opinions

of our businessmen precisely where they suppose their immediate pecuniary advantage is found?

[on the presidency] I believe I shall buy or rent a house near here where I can go and be away from this cursed constant grind.

[remark made to Franklin D. Roosevelt as a boy] Franklin, I hope you never become President.

This office seeking is a disease. . . . It is even catching.

Party honesty is party expediency.

The other side can have a monopoly of all the dirt in this campaign.

No man has ever yet been hanged for breaking the spirit of a law.

I mistake the American people if they favor the odious doctrine that there is no such thing as international morality; that there is one law for a strong nation and another for a weak one.

Whatever you do, tell the truth.

Men and times change—but principles—never.

[last words] I have tried so hard to do right.

Benjamin Harrison

Born August 20, 1833—Died March 13, 1901
23rd President, 1889–1893 ★ Republican

I want it understood that I am the grandson of nobody. I believe that every man should stand on his own merits.

Have you not learned that not stocks or bonds or stately homes, or products of mill or field are our country? It is the splendid thought that is in our minds.

We must not forget that it is often easier to assemble armies than it is to assemble army revenues.

We Americans have no commission from God to police the world.

With capability for war on land and on sea unexcelled by any nation in the world, we are smitten by the love of peace.

Vacillation and inconsistency are as incompatible with successful diplomacy as they are with the national dignity.

I believe also in the American opportunity which puts the starry sky above every boy's head, and sets his foot upon a ladder which he may climb until his strength gives out.

The manner by which women are treated is a good criterion to judge the true state of society. If we know but this one feature in a character of a nation, we may easily judge the rest, for as society advances, the true character of women is discovered.

The Yankee intermingles with the Illinoisian, the Hoosier with the Sucker, and the people of the South with them all; and it is this commingling which gives that unity which marks the American nation.

The law, the will of the majority expressed in orderly, constitutional methods, is the only king to which we bow.

Unlike many other people less happy, we give our devotion to a government, to its Constitution, to its flag, and not to men.

The indiscriminate denunciation of the rich is mischievous. It perverts the mind, poisons the heart and furnishes an excuse to crime. No poor man was ever made richer or happier by it. Not what a man has, but what he is, settles his class.

The community that by concert, open or secret, among its citizens denies a portion of its members their plain rights under the law has severed the only safe bond of social order and prosperity. The evil works, from a bad center, both ways.

All those fires of industry which I saw through the South were lighted at the funeral pyre of slavery.

Shall the prejudices and paralysis of slavery continue to hang upon the skirts of progress?

I do not know whether it is prejudice or not, but I always have a very high opinion of a state whose chief product is corn.

Public opinion is the most potent monarch this world knows.

Perhaps no emotion cools sooner than that of gratitude.

Great lives do not go out. They go on.

William McKinley
Born January 29, 1843—Died September 14, 1901
25th President, 1897–1901 ★ Republican

The ideals of yesterday are the truths of today.

Let us ever remember that our interest is in concord not in conflict, and our real eminence as a nation lies in the victories of peace, not those of war.

Our differences are politics. Our agreements are principles.

For labor a short day is better than a short dollar.

[on the presidency, after two years in office] I have had enough of it, heaven knows. I have had responsibilities enough to kill any man.

The free man cannot be long an ignorant man.

We cannot gamble with anything so sacred as money.

Liberty to make our laws does not give us license to break them.

[on the condition of the U.S. military] The Spanish fleet is in Cuban waters and we haven't enough ammunition on the Atlantic seacoast to fire a salute.

We need Hawaii just as much and a good deal more than we did California. It is Manifest Destiny.

That's all a man can hope for during his lifetime—to set an example—and when he is dead, to be an inspiration for history.

Theodore Roosevelt
Born October 27, 1858—Died January 6, 1919
26th President, 1901–1909 ★ Republican

[on the presidency] It is fine to feel one's hand guiding great machinery.

The White House is a bully pulpit.

Under government ownership corruption can flourish just as rankly as under private ownership.

Congress does from a third to a half of what I think is the minimum that it ought to do, and I am profoundly grateful that I get as much.

The things that will destroy America are prosperity-at-any-price, peace-at-any-price, safety-first instead of duty-first, the love of soft living and the get-rich-quick theory of life.

Don't hit at all if it's honorably possible to avoid hitting; but *never* hit soft!

A nation is not wholly admirable unless in times of stress it will go to war for a great ideal wholly unconnected with its immediate national interest.

The reactionary is always willing to take a progressive attitude on any issue that is dead.

A typical vice of American politics is the avoidance of saying anything real on real issues.

No people ever yet benefited by riches if their prosperity corrupted their virtue.

I never take a step in foreign policy unless I am assured that I shall be able eventually to carry out my will by force.

I took the canal zone and let Congress debate, and while the debate goes on the canal does also.

My success so far has only been won by absolute indifference to my future career.

The two great evils in the execution of our criminal laws today are sentimentality and technicality.

Wealth should be the servant not the master of the people.

Oh, if I could only be President and Congress, too, for just ten minutes.

Stand the gaff, play fair; be a good man to camp out with.

A great democracy must be progressive or it will soon cease to be a great democracy.

I wish that all Americans would realize that American politics is world politics.

Order without liberty and liberty without order are equally destructive.

There can be no delusion more fatal to the nation than the delusion that the standard of profits, of business prosperity, is sufficient in judging any business or political question.

The Constitution was made for the people and not the people for the Constitution.

There is a homely adage which runs, "Speak softly and carry a big stick; you will go far." If the American nation will speak softly and yet build and keep at a pitch of the highest training a thoroughly efficient navy, the Monroe Doctrine will go far.

It is difficult to make our material condition better by the best law, but it is easy enough to ruin it by bad laws.

No people is wholly civilized where a distinction is drawn between stealing an office and stealing a purse.

Actions speak louder than words.

The government is us: we are the government, you and I.

The leader works in the open and the boss in covert. The leader leads, and the boss drives.

There can be no effective control of corporations while their political activity remains.

A muttonhead, after an education at West Point—or Harvard—is a muttonhead still.

The American people abhor a vacuum.

Probably the greatest harm done by vast wealth is the harm that we of moderate means do ourselves when we let the vices of envy and hatred enter deep into our own natures.

There is only one quality worse than hardness of heart and that is softness of head.

Power undirected by high purpose spells calamity; and high purpose by itself is utterly useless if the power to put it into effect is lacking.

A man who has never gone to school may steal from a freight car; but if he has a university education, he may steal the whole railroad.

Americanism is a question of principle, of purpose, of idealism, or character; it is not a matter of birthplace or creed or line of descent.

This country will not be a good place for any of us to live in unless we make it a good place for all of us to live in.

Do what you can where you are with what you've got.

Whenever you are asked if you can do a job, tell 'em, "Certainly I can!" Then get busy and find out how to do it.

Keep your eyes on the stars, and your feet on the ground.

Far better it is to dare mighty things, to win glorious triumphs, even though checkered by failure, than to take rank with those poor spirits who neither enjoy much nor suffer much, because they live in the gray twilight that knows not victory nor defeat.

Every reform movement has a lunatic fringe.

Peace is generally good in itself, but it is never the highest good unless it comes as the hand-maid of righteousness; and it becomes a very evil thing if it serves merely as a mask for cowardice and sloth, or as an instrument to further the ends of despotism or anarchy.

A man who is good enough to shed his blood for his country is good enough to be given a square deal afterwards. More than that no man is entitled to, and less than that no man shall have.

I wish to preach, not the doctrine of ignoble ease, but the doctrine of the strenuous life.

No man is above the law and no man is below it; nor do we ask any man's permission when we require him to obey it.

No man needs sympathy because he has to work. . . . Far and away the best prize that life offers is the chance to work hard at work worth doing.

To waste, destroy our natural resources, to skin and exhaust the land instead of using it so as to increase its usefulness, will result in undermining in the days of our children the very prosperity which we ought by right to hand down to them amplified and developed.

The first requisite of a good citizen in this republic of ours is that he shall be able and willing to pull his weight.

The men with the muckrakes are often indispensable to the well-being of society; but only if they know when to stop raking the muck, and look upward to the celestial crown above them, to the crown of worthy endeavor.

The most successful politician is he who says what everybody is thinking most often and in the loudest voice.

You have got to have the same interest in public affairs as in private affairs, or you cannot keep this country what this country should be.

When you play, play hard; when you work, don't play at all.

No man is justified in doing evil on the ground of expediency.

Nine-tenths of wisdom consists in being wise in time.

No President ever enjoyed himself in the presidency as much as I did.

William Howard Taft

Born September 15, 1857—Died March 8, 1930
27th President, 1909–1913 ★ Republican

Well, now I'm in the White House, I'm not going to be pushed around any more.

You cannot have a decent government unless the majority exercise the self-restraint that men with great power ought to exercise.

I hate to use the patronage as a club unless I have to.

Machine politics and the spoils system are as much an enemy of a proper and efficient government system of civil service as the boll weevil is of the cotton crop.

We often . . . find the law more honored in the breach than in the observance.

The President cannot make clouds to rain and cannot make the corn to grow, he cannot make business good; although when these things occur, political parties do claim some credit for the good things that have happened in this way.

I have come to the conclusion that the major part of the work of a President is to increase the gate receipts of expositions and fairs and bring tourists into town.

There is a well-known aphorism that men are different, but all husbands are alike. The same idea may be paraphrased with respect to Congressmen. Congressmen are different, but when in opposition to an administration they are very much alike in their attitude and in their speeches.

Someone has said, "Let me make the ballads of the country, and I care not who makes the laws." One might also say, paraphrasing this, "Let anyone make the laws of the country, if I can construe them."

We live in a stage of politics, where legislators seem to regard the passage of laws as much more important than the results of their enforcement.

The world is not going to be saved by legislation, and is really benefited by an occasional two years of respite from the panacea and magic that many modern schools of politicians seem to think are to be found in the words, "Be it enacted."

In the days before the present civil service law, a sense of obligation to the President for the places held made practically all the civil employees his political henchmen.

Next to the right of liberty, the right of property

is the most important individual right guaranteed by the Constitution and the one which, united with that of personal liberty, has contributed more to the growth of civilization than any other institution established by the human race.

I am afraid I am a constant disappointment to my party. The fact of the matter is, the longer I am President the less of a party man I seem to become.

I'll be damned if I am not getting tired of this. It seems to be the profession of a President simply to hear other people talk.

Woodrow Wilson
Born December 28, 1856—Died February 3, 1924
28th President, 1913–1921 ★ Democrat

It is not men that interest or disturb me primarily; it is ideas. Ideas live; men die.

Uncompromising thought is the luxury of the closeted recluse.

I would never read a book if it were at all possible for me to talk half an hour with the man who wrote it.

If you want to make enemies, try to change something.

Responsibility is proportionate to opportunity.

You are not here merely to make a living. You are here in order to enable the world to live more amply, with greater vision, with a finer spirit of hope and achievement. You are here to enrich the world, and you impoverish yourself if you forget the errand.

I had rather have everybody on my side than be armed to the teeth.

The literary gift is a very dangerous gift to possess if you are not telling the truth, and I would a great deal rather, for my part, have a man stumble in his speech than to feel he was so exceedingly smooth that he had better be watched both day and night.

I have always been among those who believed that the greatest freedom of speech was the greatest safety, because if a man is a fool, the best thing to do is encourage him to advertise the fact by speaking.

Never murder a man who is committing suicide.

The Constitution was not made to fit us like a straitjacket. In its elasticity lies its chief greatness.

A conservative is one who makes no changes and consults his grandmother when in doubt.

The presidential office is not a rosewater affair. This is an office in which a man must put on his war paint.

The seed of revolution is repression.

No peace can last, or ought to last, which does not recognize and accept the principle that governments derive all their just powers from the consent of the governed, and that no right anywhere exists to hand peoples from sovereignty to sovereignty as if they were property.

It is a fearful thing to lead this great peaceful people into war, into the most terrible and disastrous of all wars, civilization itself seeming to be in the balance.

The world must be made safe for democracy. Its peace must be planted upon the tested foundations of political liberty. We have no selfish ends to serve. We desire no conquest, no dominion. We seek no indemnities for ourselves, no material compensation for the sacrifices we shall freely make.

If I cannot retain my moral influence over a man except by occasionally knocking him down, if that is the only basis upon which he will respect me, then for the sake of his soul I have got occasionally to knock him down.

Whatever may be said against the chewing of

tobacco, this at least can be said of it, that it gives a man time to think between sentences.

The cure for bad politics is the same as the cure for tuberculosis. It is living in the open.

Publicity is one of the purifying elements of politics. Nothing checks all the bad practices of politics like public exposure. An Irishman, seen digging around the wall of a house, was asked what he was doing. He answered, "Faith, I am letting the dark out of the cellar." Now, that's exactly what we want to do.

It's harder for a leader to be born in a palace than to be born in a cabin.

People will endure their tyrants for years, but they tear their deliverers to pieces if a millennium is not created immediately.

You must act in your friend's interest whether it pleases him or not; the object of love is to serve, not to win.

The Constitution of the United States is not a mere lawyers' document; it is a vehicle of life, and its spirit is always the spirit of the age.

There is something better, if possible, that a man can give than his life. That is his living spirit to a service that is not easy, to resist counsels that are hard to resist, to stand against purposes that are difficult to stand against.

There is here a great melting pot in which we must compound a precious metal. That metal is the metal of nationality.

[on World War I] Our whole duty, for the present at any rate, is summed up in this motto: "America first."

I am not one of those who believe that a great standing army is the means of maintaining peace, because if you build up a great profession those who form parts of it want to exercise their profession.

America is not a mere body of traders; it is a body of free men. Our greatness is built upon our freedom—is moral, not material. We have a great ardor for gain; but we have a deep passion for the rights of man.

I have sometimes heard men say politics must have nothing to do with business, and I have often wished that business had nothing to do with politics.

When the representatives of "Big Business" think of the people, they do not include themselves.

Life does not consist in thinking, it consists in acting.

One cool judgment is worth a thousand hasty

councils. The thing to do is to supply light and not heat.

We are citizens of the world; and the tragedy of our times is that we do not know this.

If you think too much about being reelected, it is very difficult to be worth reelecting.

A man's rootage is more important than his leafage.

If you would be a leader of men, you must lead your own generation, not the next.

The President is a superior kind of slave, and must content himself with the reflection that the *kind* is superior!

If you think about what you ought to do for other people, your character will take care of itself.

By "radical" I understand one who goes too far; by "conservative" one who does not go far enough; by "reactionary" one who won't go at all. I suppose I must be a "progressive," which I take to be one who insists on recognizing new facts, adjusting policies to facts and circumstances as they arise.

Every man who takes office in Washington either grows or swells, and when I give a man an office, I watch him carefully to see whether he is swelling or growing. The mischief of it is that when they swell, they do not swell enough to burst.

There is a price which is too great to pay for peace, and that price can be put in one word. One cannot pay the price of self-respect.

Only a peace between equals can last.

Things get very lonely in Washington sometimes. The real voice of the great people of America sometimes sounds faint and distant in that strange city. You hear politics until you wish that both parties were smothered in their own gas.

The law that will work is merely the summing up in legislative form of the moral judgment that the community has already reached.

Justice has nothing to do with expediency. Justice has nothing to do with any temporary standard whatever. It is rooted and grounded in the fundamental instincts of humanity.

Peace like charity begins at home.

Jefferson's Declaration of Independence is a practical document for the use of practical men. It is not a thesis for philosophers, but a whip for tyrants; it is not a theory of government but a program of action.

The use of a university is to make young gentlemen as unlike their fathers as possible.

I have always summed up for myself individual liberty and business liberty and every other kind of liberty in the phrase that is common in the sporting world—"A free field and no favor."

Hunger does not breed reform; it breeds madness, and all the ugly distempers that make an ordered life impossible.

Business underlies everything in our national life, including our spiritual life. Witness the fact that in the Lord's Prayer, the first petition is for daily bread. No one can worship God or love his neighbor on an empty stomach.

A nation is as great, and only as great, as her rank and file.

Caution is the confidential agent of selfishness.

Self-determination is not a mere phrase. It is an imperative principle of action, which statesmen will henceforth ignore at their peril.

Character is a by-product; it is produced in the great manufacture of daily duty.

High society is for those who have stopped working and no longer have anything important to do.

Our American merchant ships must be protected by our American navy. It can never be doubted that the goods *will* be delivered by this nation, whose navy believes in the tradition of "Damn the torpedoes; full speed ahead!"

[on the presidency] [It requires] the constitution of an athlete, the patience of a mother, the endurance of the early Christian.

Warren Gamaliel Harding
Born November 2, 1865—Died August 2, 1923
29th President, 1921–1923 ★ Republican

I don't know much about Americanism, but it's a damn good word with which to carry an election.

Ambition is a commendable attribute, without which no man succeeds. Only inconsiderate ambition imperils.

I am a man of limited talents, from a small town. I do not seem to grasp that I am President.

My God, this is a hell of a job! I have no trouble with my enemies. I can take care of my enemies all right. But my damn friends, my goddamn friends . . . they are the ones that keep me walking the floor nights.

The White House is a prison. I can't get away

from the men who dog my footsteps. I am in jail.

In the great fulfillment we must have a citizenship less concerned about what the government can do for it and more anxious about what it can do for the nation.

I have said to the people we mean to have less government in business as well as more business in government.

Stabilize America first, prosper America first, think of America first and exalt America first.

Frankly, being President is rather an unattractive business unless one relishes the exercise of power. That is a thing which has never greatly appealed to me.

Calvin Coolidge
Born July 4, 1872—Died January 5, 1933
30th President, 1923–1929 ★ Republican

I think the American public wants a solemn ass as President and I think I'll go along with them.

I shall always consider it the highest tribute to my administration that the opposition have based so little of their criticism on what I have really said and done.

It is difficult for men in high office to avoid the malady of self-delusion. They are always surrounded by worshippers. They are constantly, and for the most part sincerely, assured of their greatness.

It is a great advantage to a President, and a major source of safety to the country, for him to know that he is not a great man.

I have noticed that nothing I never said ever did me any harm.

People who've had a hanging in the family don't like to talk about rope.

A lost article invariably shows up after you replace it.

Never go out to meet trouble. If you will just sit still, nine cases out of ten, someone will intercept it before it reaches you.

The fundamental precept of liberty is toleration.

There is no force so democratic as the force of an ideal.

One with the law is a majority.

The right thing to do never requires any subterfuge, it is always simple and direct.

No person was ever honored for what he received. Honor has been the reward for what he gave.

Press on: nothing in the world can take the place of perseverance. Talent will not; nothing is more common than unsuccessful men with talent. Genius will not; unrewarded genius is almost a proverb. Education will not; the world is full of educated derelicts. Persistence and determination alone are omnipotent.

The country would not be a land of opportunity, America would not be America, if the people were shackled with government monopolies.

The moment the government engages in buying and selling, by that act it is fixing prices.

Civilization and profits go hand in hand.

The chief business of America is business.

Prosperity is only an instrument to be used, not a deity to be worshipped.

There is no dignity quite so impressive, and no independence quite so important, as living within your means.

The power to tax is the power to destroy. A government which lays taxes on the people not required by urgent public necessity and sound public policy is not a protector of liberty, but an instrument of tyranny.

Nothing is easier than spending public money. It does not appear to belong to anybody. The temptation is overwhelming to bestow it on somebody.

I have in mind that the taxpayers are the stockholders of the business corporation of the United States, and that if this business is showing a surplus of receipts the taxpayer should share therein in some material way that will be of immediate benefit.

It is because in their hours of timidity the Congress becomes subservient to the importunities of organized minorities that the President comes more and more to stand as the champion of the rights of the whole country.

It is the duty of a citizen not only to observe the law but to let it be known that he is opposed to its violation.

The nation which forgets its defenders will itself be forgotten.

Patriotism is easy to understand in America. It means looking out for yourself by looking out for your country.

No nation ever had an army large enough to guarantee it against attack in time of peace, or insure it victory in time of war.

War is the rule of force. Peace is the reign of law.

[on World War I] What the end of the four

years of carnage meant those who remember it will never forget and those who do not can never be told.

[on the presidency] You have to stand every day three or four hours of visitors. Nine-tenths of them want something they ought not to have. If you keep dead-still they will run down in three or four minutes. If you even cough or smile they will start up all over again.

[on the 1919 Boston police strike] There is no right to strike against the public safety by any-body, anywhere, any time.

Perhaps one of the most important accomplishments of my administration has been minding my own business.

Herbert Clark Hoover
Born August 10, 1874—Died October 20, 1964
31st President, 1929–1933 ★ Republican

No public man can be just a little crooked.

Once upon a time my political opponents honored me as possessing the fabulous intellectual and economic power by which I created a world-wide depression all by myself.

Even if security from the cradle to the grave could eliminate the risks of life, it would be a dead hand on the creative spirit of our people.

Blessed are the young, for they shall inherit the national debt.

The worst evil of disregard for some law is that it destroys respect for all law.

It is just as important that business keep out of government as that government keep out of business.

No nation or individual has been able to squander itself into prosperity.

Votes are the professional politicians' idea of the food of gods, which is kept in pork barrels.

Modern society cannot survive with the defense of Cain, "Am I my brother's keeper?"

[on the presidency] The office in such times as these makes its incumbent a repairman behind a dike. No sooner is one leak plugged up than it is necessary to dash over and stop another that has broken out. There is no end to it.

[and]

The thing I enjoyed most were visits from children. They did not want public offices.

A revered President long since dead once told me that there was no solution to this relation of the White House to the press; that there would never be a President who could satisfy the press until he was twenty years dead.

It is well to remember that the office of Chief Executive is in part a symbol of the nation, and that leaders in a nation may differ in their own house but they have instant solidarity in the presence of foreign attack.

Presidents have long since learned that one of the undisclosed articles in the Bill of Rights is that criticism and digging of political graves are reserved exclusively to members of the legislative arm.

In the Middle Ages it was the fashion to wear hair shirts to remind one's self of trouble and sin. Many years ago I concluded that a few hair shirts were part of the mental wardrobe of every man. The President differs only from other men in that he has a more extensive wardrobe.

Being a politician is a poor profession. Being a public servant is a noble one.

When there is a lack of honor in government, the morals of the whole people are poisoned.

Free speech does not live many hours after free industry and free commerce die.

One who brandishes a pistol must be prepared to shoot.

To maintain peace is as dynamic in its require-
ments as the conduct of war.

It is a paradox that every dictator has climbed to
power on the ladder of free speech. Immediately
on attaining power each dictator has suppressed
all free speech except his own.

The slogan of progress is changing from the full
dinner pail to the full garage.

[Hoover's campaign slogan] Two cars in every
garage.

There are only two occasions when Americans
respect privacy, especially in presidents. Those
are prayer and fishing.

Fishing is the chance to wash one's soul with
pure air. It brings meekness and inspiration, reduces our egotism, soothes our troubles, and
shames our wickedness. It is discipline in the
equality of men; for all men are equal before
fish.

Those who retire without some occupation can
spend their time only in talking about their ills
and pills.

The President ought to be allowed to hang two
men every year without giving any reason or ex-
planation.

Franklin Delano Roosevelt
Born January 30, 1882—Died April 12, 1945
32nd President, 1933–1945 ★ *Democrat*

The ablest man I ever met is the man you think you are.

Let me assert my firm belief that the only thing we have to fear is fear itself—nameless, unreasoning, unjustified terror which paralyzes needed efforts to convert retreat into advance.

Never underestimate a man who overestimates himself.

We all know the story of the unfortunate chameleon which turned brown when placed on a brown rug, and turned red when placed on a red rug, but who died a tragic death when they put him on a Scotch plaid.

When you get to the end of your rope, tie a knot and hang on.

[on public speaking] Be sincere; be brief; be seated.

Presidents do make mistakes, but the immortal Dante tells us that divine justice weighs the sins of the cold-blooded and the sins of the warm-hearted in different scales.

It's a terrible thing to look over your shoulder

when you are trying to lead—and find no one there.

These Republican leaders have not been content with attacks upon me, or my wife, or on my sons—no, not content with that, they now include my little dog, Fala. Unlike the members of my family, he resents this.

A government can be no better than the public opinion which sustains it.

Our Constitution is so simple and practical that it is possible always to meet extraordinary needs by changes in emphasis and arrangement without loss of essential form.

Democracy is not a static thing. It is an everlasting march.

The saving grace of America lies in the fact that the overwhelming majority of Americans are possessed of two great qualities—a sense of humor and a sense of proportion.

If we can "boondoggle" ourselves out of this depression, that word is going to be enshrined in the hearts of the American people for years to come.

We can afford all that we need; but we cannot afford all we want.

Happiness lies not in the mere possession of

money; it lies in the joy of achievement, in the thrill of creative effort.

It is an unfortunate human failing that a full pocketbook often groans more loudly than an empty stomach.

Private enterprise is ceasing to be free enterprise.

I see one-third of a nation ill-housed, ill-clad, ill-nourished.

The test of our progress is not whether we add more to the abundance of those who have much; it is whether we provide enough for those who have too little.

We have always known that heedless self-interest was bad morals; we know now that is bad economics.

Here is my principle: Taxes shall be levied according to ability to pay. That is the only American principle.

I pledge you—I pledge myself—to a new deal for the American people.

In the field of world policy, I would dedicate this nation to the policy of the good neighbor . . . the neighbor who respects his obligations and respects the sanctity of his agreements in and with a world of neighbors.

I should like to have it said of my first adminis-tration that in it the forces of selfishness and of lust for power met their match. . . . I should like to have it said of my second administration that in it these forces met their master.

Do we really have to assume that nations can find no better methods of realizing their des-tinies than those which were used by the Huns and Vandals fifteen hundred years ago?

There is a mysterious cycle in human events. To some generations much is given. Of others much is expected. This generation of Americans has a rendezvous with destiny.

We must be the great arsenal of democracy.

A just war in the long run is far better for a man's soul than the most prosperous peace.

I have seen war. I hate war.

The truth is found when men are free to pursue it.

As a nation we may take pride in the fact that we are soft-hearted; but we cannot afford to be soft-headed. We must always be wary of those who with sounding brass and a tinkling cymbal preach the "ism" of appeasement. We must es-pecially beware of that small group of selfish men who would clip the wings of the American eagle in order to feather their own nests.

A radical is a man with both feet firmly planted—in the air. A conservative is a man with two perfectly good legs who, however, has never learned to walk forward. A reactionary is a somnambulist walking backwards. A liberal is a man who uses his legs and his hands at the behest of his head.

When peace has been broken anywhere, the peace of all countries everywhere is in danger.

Those who would give up essential liberty to purchase a little temporary safety deserve neither liberty nor safety.

In the future days, which we seek to make secure, we look forward to a world founded upon four essential human freedoms. The first is freedom of speech and expression—everywhere in the world. The second is freedom of every person to worship God in his own way—everywhere in the world. The third is freedom from want . . . everywhere in the world. The fourth is freedom from fear . . . anywhere in the world.

People who are hungry and out of a job are the stuff of which dictatorships are made.

The ultimate failures of dictatorship cost

humanity far more than any temporary failures of democracy.

We . . . would rather die on our feet than live on our knees.

Yesterday, December 7, 1941—a date which will live in infamy—the United States of America was suddenly and deliberately attacked by naval and air forces of the Empire of Japan.

[on the presidency] The first twelve years are the hardest.

Harry S Truman
Born May 8, 1884–Died December 26, 1972
33rd President, 1945–1953 ★ Democrat

It was said in the First World War that the French fought for their country, the British fought for freedom of the seas, and the Americans fought for souvenirs.

The menace of communism lies primarily in those areas of American life where the promise of democracy remains unfulfilled.

I learned that a leader is a man who has the ability to get other people to do what they don't want to do, and like it.

Intense feeling often obscures the truth.

Being too good is apt to be uninteresting.

If you want to live like a Republican, you've got to vote for a Democrat.

A President either is constantly on top of events, or if he hesitates, events will soon be on top of him.

The President is the representative of the whole nation and he's the only lobbyist that all one hundred and sixty million people in this country have.

Sixteen hours ago an American airplane dropped one bomb on Hiroshima. . . . The force from which the sun draws its powers has been used against those who brought war to the Far East.

There is no exaltation in the office of the President of the United States—sorrow is the proper word.

When a leader is in the Democratic party he's a boss; when he's in the Republican party he's a leader.

Anything that is sent up to the Senate and House with my name on it will quiver a couple of times and then turn over and die.

If you don't have a sense of humor, you're in a hell of a fix when you are President of the United States.

It takes only one nation to make war. But it takes two or more to make peace.

Being a President is like riding a tiger. A man has to keep on riding or be swallowed.

I have appointed a Secretary of Semantics—a most important post. He is to furnish me with forty to fifty dollar words. Tell me how to say yes and no in the same sentence without a contradiction. He is to tell me the combination of words that will put me against inflation in San Francisco and for it in New York.

The President hears a hundred voices telling him that he is the greatest man in the world. He must listen carefully indeed to hear the one voice that tells him he is not.

A politician is a man who understands government, and it takes a politician to run a government. A statesman is a politician who's been dead ten or fifteen years.

Isolationism is the road to war. Worse than that, isolationism is the road to defeat in war.

I'm going to fight hard. I'm going to give them hell.

Liberty does not make all men perfect nor all society secure. But it has provided more solid progress and happiness and decency for more people than any other philosophy of government in history.

These polls that the Republican candidate is putting out are like pills designed to lull the voters into sleeping on Election Day. You ought to call them sleeping polls.

If you tell Congress everything about the world situation, they get hysterical. If you tell them nothing, they go fishing.

A President may dismiss the abuse of scoundrels, but to be denounced by honest men honestly outraged is a test of greatness that none but the strongest men can survive.

About the meanest thing you can say about a man is that he means well.

Three things ruin a man. Power, money, and women. I never wanted power. I never had any money, and the only woman in my life is up at the house right now.

If there is one basic element in our Constitution, it is civilian control of the military.

In my opinion eight years as President is enough and sometimes too much for any man to serve in that capacity. There is a lure in power. It can get into a man's blood just as gambling and lust for money have been known to do.

Our allies are the millions who hunger and thirst after righteousness.

I am getting ready to see Stalin and Churchill and it is a chore. I have to take my tuxedo, tails, preacher coat, high hat, low hat and hard hat.

When I hear Republicans say I'm doing all right, I know damned well I'm wrong.

These men who live in the past remind me of a toy . . . a small wooden bird called the Floogie Bird. Around the Floogie Bird's neck is a label reading: "I fly backwards. I don't care where I'm going. I just want to see where I've been."

If you can't convince them, confuse them.

Men make history and not the other way around. In periods where there is no leadership, society stands still.

The Republican Party either corrupts its liberals or it expels them.

GOP these days means just one thing: "Grand Old Platitudes."

The Republicans stand four-square for the American home—but not for housing.

It's a recession when your neighbor loses his job, it's a depression when you lose your own.

I found the best way to give advice to your

children is to find out what they want and then advise them to do it.

My favorite animal is the mule. He has more horse sense than a horse. He knows when to stop eating—and he knows when to stop working.

All the President is, is a glorified public relations man who spends his time flattering, kissing, and kicking people to get them to do what they are supposed to do anyway.

It was in 1948, and we were holding an enthusiastic meeting [in Seattle] when some man with a great big voice cried from the galleries, "Give 'em hell, Harry!" I told him at that time, and I have been repeating it ever since, that I have never deliberately given anybody hell. I just tell the truth on the opposition—and they think it's hell.

[hand-lettered sign on Truman's desk] The buck stops here.

If you can't stand the heat, get out of the kitchen.

My choice early in life was either to be a piano-player in a whorehouse or a politician. And to tell the truth, there's hardly any difference.

I always quote an epitaph on a tombstone in a

cemetery in Tombstone, Arizona: "Here lies Jack Williams. He done his damnedest." I think that is the greatest epitaph a man can have . . . and that is what I have tried to do.

Dwight David Eisenhower
Born October 14, 1890—Died March 28, 1969
34th President, 1953–1961 ★ Republican

Neither a wise man nor a brave man lies down on the tracks of history to wait for the train of the future to run over him.

In the service, when a man gives you his word, his word is binding. In politics, you never know.

The opportunist thinks of me and today. The statesman thinks of us and tomorrow.

You know, once in a while I get to the point, with everybody staring at me, where I want to go back indoors and pull down the curtains.

There are a number of things wrong with Washington. One of them is that everyone has been too long away from home.

No one should be appointed to political office if he is a seeker after it.

Patronage is almost a wicked word. By itself it could well-nigh defeat democracy.

Accomplishment will prove to be a journey, not a destination.

I would rather try to persuade a man to go along, because once I have persuaded him he will stick. If I scare him, he will stay just as long as he is scared, and then he is gone.

Whatever America hopes to bring to pass in this world must first come to pass in the heart of America.

There can be no such thing as Fortress America. If ever we were reduced to the isolationism implied by that term we would occupy a prison, not a fortress.

What counts is not the size of the dog in the fight but the size of the fight in the dog.

The only way to win World War III is to prevent it.

In the councils of government, we must guard against the acquisition of unwarranted influence, whether sought or unsought, by the military-industrial complex. The potential for the disastrous rise of misplaced power exists and will persist.

Dollars and guns are no substitute for brains and willpower.

[on the atomic bomb] It is not enough to take

this weapon out of the hands of soldiers. It must be put into the hands of those who will know how to strip its military casing and adapt it to the arts of peace.

In the final choice a soldier's pack is not so heavy a burden as a prisoner's chains.

Men acquainted with the battlefield will not be found among the numbers that glibly talk of another war.

War is a contest, and you finally get to a point where you are talking merely about race suicide, and nothing else.

Every gun that is made, every warship launched, every rocket fired signifies, in the final sense, a theft from those who hunger and are not fed, those who are cold and are not clothed.

Under the cloud of threatening war, it is humanity hanging from a cross of iron.

I think that people want peace so much that one of these days governments had better get out of the way and let them have it.

Peace signifies more than the stilling of guns, easing the sorrow of war. More than escape from death, it is a way of life. More than a haven for the weary, it is a hope for the brave.

We cherish our friendship with all nations that

would be free. And when, in time of want or peril, they ask our help, they may honorably receive it; for we no more seek to buy their sovereignty than we would sell our own.

Unless we can put things in the hands of people who are starving to death we can never lick Communism.

[on Senator Joe McCarthy] I just won't get into a pissing contest with that skunk.

Don't join the book burners. Don't think you're going to conceal faults by concealing evidence that they ever existed.

The search for a scapegoat is the easiest of all hunting expeditions.

An intellectual is a man who takes more words than necessary to tell more than he knows.

A people that values its privileges above its principles soon loses both.

The final battle against intolerance is to be fought—not in the chambers of any legislature—but in the hearts of men.

The older I get, the more wisdom I find in the ancient rule of taking first things first—a process which often reduces the most complex human problems to manageable proportions.

Farming looks mighty easy when your plow is a pencil, and you're a thousand miles from a cornfield.

People talk about the middle of the road as though it were unacceptable. Actually, all human problems, excepting morals, come into the gray areas. . . . The middle of the road is all of the usable surface. The extremes, right and left, are in the gutters.

There is one thing about being President—nobody can tell you when to sit down.

John Fitzgerald Kennedy
Born May 29, 1917—Died November 22, 1963
35th President, 1961–1963 ★ Democrat

I have just received the following telegram from my generous daddy. It says, "Dear Jack: Don't buy a single vote more than is necessary. I'll be damned if I'm going to pay for a landslide."

When we got into office, the thing that surprised me most was to find that things were just as bad as we'd been saying they were.

I don't think the intelligence reports are all that hot. Some days I get more out of *The New York Times.*

It is much easier in many ways for me—and for other Presidents, I think, who felt the same way—when Congress is not in town.

[remark made at a 1962 White House dinner honoring Nobel Laureates] I think this is the most extraordinary collection of talent, of human knowledge, that has ever been gathered together at the White House—with the possible exception of when Thomas Jefferson dined alone.

Mothers all want their sons to grow up to be President but they don't want them to become politicians in the process.

[on becoming a World War II hero] It was involuntary. They sank my boat.

Those of you who regard my profession of political life with some disdain should remember that it made it possible for me to move from being an obscure lieutenant in the United States Navy to Commander in Chief in fourteen years with very little technical competence.

Politics is like football. If you see daylight, go through the hole.

[describing himself] An idealist without illusions.

It has recently been observed that whether I serve one or two terms in the presidency, I will find myself at the end of that period at what might be called the awkward age—too old to begin a career and too young to write my memoirs.

Washington is a city of southern efficiency and northern charm.

What we need now in this nation, more than atomic power, or air power, or financial, industrial, or even manpower, is brain power. The dinosaur was bigger and stronger than anyone else—but he was also dumber. And look what happened to him.

Of those to whom much is given, much is required.

And so, my fellow Americans: ask not what your country can do for you—ask what you can do for your country.

We stand today at the edge of a new frontier—the frontier of the 1960s—a frontier of unknown opportunities and perils—a frontier of unfulfilled hopes and threats.

The mere absence of war is not peace.

The risks inherent in disarmament pale in comparison to the risks inherent in an unlimited arms race.

Those who make peaceful revolution impossible will make violent revolution inevitable.

Unconditional war can no longer lead to unconditional victory. Mankind must put an end to war or war will put an end to mankind.

We have the power to make this the best generation of mankind in the history of the world—or to make it the last.

War will exist until that distant day when the conscientious objector enjoys the same reputation and prestige that the warrior does today.

Victory has a hundred fathers, but defeat is an orphan.

The same revolutionary beliefs for which our forebears fought are still at issue around the globe—the belief that the rights of man come not from the generosity of the state but from the hand of God.

Liberty without learning is always in peril and learning without liberty is always in vain.

If we cannot now end our differences, at least we can help make the world safe for diversity.

Let us never negotiate out of fear. But let us never fear to negotiate.

Too often we . . . enjoy the comfort of opinion without the discomfort of thought.

The great enemy of the truth is very often not the lie—deliberate, contrived, and dishonest—but the myth—persistent, persuasive, and unrealistic.

In the past, those who foolishly sought power by riding the back of the tiger ended up inside.

Our strength and our hope is the United Nations, and I see little merit in the impatience of those who would abandon this imperfect world instrument because they dislike our imperfect world.

I know something about Mr. Khrushchev. . . . Mr. Khrushchev himself, it is said, told the story about the Russian who began to run through the Kremlin, shouting, "Khrushchev is a fool. Khrushchev is a fool." He was sentenced, he said, to twenty-three years in prison: three for insulting the Party Secretary, and twenty for revealing a state secret.

No one has been barred on account of his race from fighting or dying for America—there are no "white" or "colored" signs on the foxholes or graveyards of battle.

We cannot expect that all nations will adopt like systems, for conformity is the jailer of freedom and the enemy of growth.

Sincerity is always subject to proof.

History is a relentless master. It has no present, only the past rushing into the future. To try to hold fast is to be swept aside.

You can always survive a mistake in domestic affairs, but you may get killed by one made in foreign policy.

The courage of life is often a less dramatic spectacle than the courage of a final moment; but it is no less than a magnificent mixture of triumph and tragedy.

Lyndon Baines Johnson
Born August 27, 1908—Died January 22, 1973
36th President, 1963–1969 ★ Democrat

In 1790, the nation which had fought a revolution against taxation without representation discovered that some of its citizens weren't much happier about taxation with representation.

The Secretary of Labor is in charge of finding you a job, the Secretary of the Treasury is in charge of taking half the money away from you, and the Attorney General is in charge of suing you for the other half.

Politics is the art of the possible.

There is but one way for a President to deal with the Congress, and that is continuously, incessantly, and without interruption.

One lesson you'd better learn if you want to be in politics is that you never go out on a golf course and beat the President.

You ain't learnin' nothin' when you're talkin'.

The presidency has made every man who occupied it, no matter how small, bigger than he was: and no matter how big, not big enough for its demands.

Words wound. But as a veteran of twelve years in the U.S. Senate, I happily attest they do not kill.

If you're in politics and you can't tell when you walk into a room who's for you and who's against you, then you're in the wrong line of work.

Law is the greatest human invention. All the rest give him mastery over his world, but law gives him mastery over himself.

We did not choose to be the guardians at the gate. But there is no one else.

War is always the same. It is young men dying in the fullness of their promise. It is trying to kill a man that you do not even know well enough to hate. Therefore, to know war is to know that there is still madness in this world.

We must be constantly prepared for the worst and constantly acting for the best—strong enough to win a war and wise enough to prevent one.

It is easier today to buy a destructive weapon, a gun, in a hardware store, than it is to vote.

Free speech, free press, free religion, the right of free assembly, yes, the right of petition . . . they are still radical ideas.

Poverty has many roots, but the tap root is ignorance.

To hunger for use and to go unused is the worst hunger of all.

The world is engaged in a race between education and chaos.

Education, more than any single force, will mold the citizen of the future. The classroom—not the trench—is the frontier of freedom.

Once we considered education a public expense; we know now that it is a public investment.

There is no Negro problem. There is no Southern problem. There is no Northern problem. There is only an American problem.

Justice means a man's hope should not be limited by the color of his skin.

Unfortunately, many Americans live on the outskirts of hope—some because of their poverty, and some because of their color, and all too many because of both. Our task is to help replace their despair with opportunity.

If we become two people—the suburban affluent and the urban poor, each filled with mistrust and fear of the other—then we shall effectively cripple each generation to come.

Giving a man a chance to work and feed his family and provide for his children does not destroy his initiative. Hunger destroys initiative. Ignorance destroys initiative. A cold and indifferent government destroys initiative.

If government is to serve any purpose it is to do for others what they are unable to do for themselves.

Until justice is blind to color, until education is unaware of race, until opportunity is unconcerned with the color of men's skins, emancipation will be a proclamation but not a fact.

This nation, this generation, in this hour, has man's first chance to build a Great Society, a place where the meaning of man's life matches the marvels of man's labor.

This administration, today, here and now, declares unconditional war on poverty in America. Our objective is total victory.

The women of America represent a reservoir of talent that is still underused. It is too often underpaid, and almost always underpromoted.

Only two things are necessary to keep a wife

happy. One is to let her think she is having her way, and the other is to let her have it.

I, who preached moderation to everyone, never practiced it myself. I didn't have ulcers; I gave them to the people who worked for me.

I strive for the best and I do the possible.

Being President is like being a jackass in a hailstorm. There's nothing to do but stand there and take it.

Richard Milhous Nixon
Born January 9, 1913—Died April 22, 1994
37th President, 1969–1974 ★ Republican

[on accepting the Republican Presidential nomination, 1968] Let us begin by committing ourselves to the truth—to see it like it is, and tell it like it is—to find the truth, to speak the truth, and to live the truth.

Voters quickly forget what a man says.

You cannot win a battle in any arena merely by defending yourself.

Neutrality where the Communists are concerned means three things: we get out; they stay in; they take over.

Communist leaders believe in Lenin's precept:

Probe with bayonets. If you encounter mush, proceed; if you encounter steel, withdraw.

Government must learn to take less from the people so that people can do more for themselves.

[on the first moon landing, July 20, 1969] For years politicians have promised the moon—I'm the first one to be able to deliver it.

A man who has never lost himself in a cause bigger than himself has missed one of life's mountaintop experiences. Only in losing himself does he find himself.

The game of life is to come up a winner, to be a success, or to achieve what we set out to do. Yet there is always the danger of failing as a human being. The lesson that most of us on this voyage never learn, but can never quite forget, is that to win is sometimes to lose.

I urged my audiences to be Lincoln Republicans: liberal in their concern for people and conservative in their respect for the rule of law.

The American defense establishment should never be a sacred cow, but on the other hand, the American military should never be anybody's scapegoat.

President Eisenhower's whole life is proof of the

stark but simple truth—that no one hates war more than one who has seen a lot of it.

Former presidents of the United States are like British kings; they have great responsibility but no power.

Government enterprise is the most inefficient and costly way of producing jobs.

The people's right to change what does not work is one of the greatest principles of our system of government.

History makes the man more than the man makes history.

The conventional way to handle a meeting at the summit like this, while the whole world is watching, is to have meetings for several days, which we will have, to have discussions and discover differences, which we will do, and then put out a weasel-worded communiqué covering up the problems.

It is time for the great silent majority of Americans to stand up and be counted.

I believe in building bridges but we should build only our end of the bridge.

With all of our differences, whenever we are confronted with a threat to our security we are not then Republicans or Democrats but

Americans; we are not then fifty states but the United States.

When you buy peace at any price it is always on the installment plan for another year.

In dealing with the environment we must learn not how to master nature but how to master ourselves, our institutions, and our technology.

If you want to make beautiful music, you must play the black and the white notes together.

I bring you Peace with Honor, not Peace with Surrender.

[in 1962, after losing the California gubernatorial race] Now that all the members of the press are so delighted I lost, I would like to make a statement. As I leave you I want you to think about how much you'll be missing. You won't have Nixon to kick around anymore because, gentlemen, this is my last press conference.

Pat and I have the satisfaction that every dime that we've got is honestly ours. I should say this, that Pat doesn't have a mink coat. But she does have a respectable Republican cloth coat, and I always tell her that she would look good in anything.

[on Checkers, the Nixons' dog] The kids, like all kids, loved the dog, and I just want to say this,

right now, that regardless of what they say about it, we are going to keep it.

The media are far more powerful than the President in creating public awareness and shaping public opinion, for the simple reason that the media always have the last word.

I'm an introvert in an extrovert's profession.

I learned a great deal from a football coach who not only taught his players how to win but also taught them that when you lose you don't quit, that when you lose you fight harder the next time.

The Chinese use two brush strokes to write the word "crisis." One brush stroke stands for danger; the other for opportunity. In a crisis, be aware of the danger—but recognize the opportunity.

[on the Watergate scandal] I felt sure that it was just a public-relations problem that only needed a public-relations solution.

[and]

There can be no whitewash in the White House.

The trouble with Republicans is that when they get into trouble, they start acting like cannibals.

Those who hate you don't win unless you hate them. And then you destroy yourself.

The finest steel has to go through the hottest fire.

When the President does it, that means it is not illegal.

Once you get into this great stream of history, you can't get out.

A man is not finished when he's defeated; he's finished when he quits.

I brought myself down. I impeached myself by resigning.

If any individual wants to be a leader and isn't controversial, that means he never stood for anything.

Gerald Rudolph Ford
Born July 14, 1913 ★ 38th President, 1974–1977
★ Republican

I was America's first instant Vice President—and now, America's first instant President. The Marine Corps Band is so confused, they don't know whether to play "Hail to the Chief" or "You've Come a Long Way, Baby."

You know all those Secret Service men you've seen around me? When I play golf, they get combat pay!

I'm a Ford, not a Lincoln.

Only eight months ago, when I last stood here, I told you I was a Ford, not a Lincoln. Tonight I say I am still a Ford, but I am not a Model T.

To me the presidency and vice-presidency were not prizes to be won but a duty to be done.

Truth is the glue that holds governments together. Compromise is the oil that makes governments go.

A government big enough to give you everything you want is a government big enough to take from you everything you have.

One of the enduring truths of the nation's capital is that bureaucrats survive.

Our inflation, our public enemy number one, will, unless whipped, destroy our country, our homes, our liberties, our property and finally our national pride as surely as will any well-armed wartime enemy.

A bronco is something that kicks and bucks, twists and turns, and very seldom goes in one direction. We have one of those things here in Washington. It's called the Congress.

If the Soviet Union and the United States can reach an agreement so that our astronauts can fit together the most intricate scientific equipment, work together and shake hands 137 miles out in space, we as statesmen have an obligation to do as well on earth.

[on his pardon of Richard Nixon] It can go on and on, or someone must write "The End" to it. I have concluded that only I can do that. And if I can, I must.

The three-martini lunch is the epitome of American efficiency. Where else can you get an earful, a bellyful and a snootful at the same time?

[on his presidency] I guess it just proves that in America anyone can be President.

James Earl Carter
Born October 1, 1924 ★ 39th President, 1977–1981
★ Democrat

America did not invent human rights. In a very real sense . . . human rights invented America.

The best way to enhance freedom in other lands is to demonstrate here that our democratic system is worthy of emulation.

We were taught that our armies were always invincible and our causes always just, only to suffer the agony of Vietnam.

We were sure that ours was a nation of the

ballot, not the bullet, until the murders of John Kennedy, Robert Kennedy, and Martin Luther King, Jr.

I have a vision of an America that is, in Bob Dylan's phrase, busy being born, not dying.

Whatever starts in California unfortunately has an inclination to spread.

I think the government ought to stay out of the prayer business.

Government is a contrivance of human wisdom to provide for human wants.

A simple and proper function of government is just to make it easy for us to do good and difficult for us to do wrong.

The tax system is a disgrace to the human race. . . . It's a scandal that a businessman can deduct his fifty-dollar lunch but a worker can't deduct the sandwich in his lunch pail.

If you fear making anyone mad, then you ultimately probe for the lowest common denominator of human achievement.

We must adjust to changing times and still hold to unchanging principles.

We should live our lives as though Christ were coming this afternoon.

I can get up at nine and be rested, or I can get up at six and be President.

I've looked on a lot of women with lust. I've committed adultery in my heart many times. This is something that God recognizes I will do—and I have done it—and God forgives me for it.

We've uncovered some embarrassing ancestors in the not too distant past. Some horse thieves, and some people killed on Saturday nights. One of my relatives, unfortunately, was even in the newspaper business.

[on his brother, Billy Carter] Billy's doing his share for the economy. He's put the beer industry back on its feet.

I have a lot of problems on my shoulders but, strangely enough, I feel better as they pile up. My main concern is propping up the people around me who tend to panic, and who might possibly have a better picture of the situation than I do.

My esteem in this country has gone up substantially. It is very nice now when people wave at me, they use all their fingers.

Ronald Wilson Reagan
Born February 6, 1911 ★ 40th President,
1981–1989 ★ Republican

Excellence does not begin in Washington.

I'm proud to be called a pig. It stands for pride, integrity, and guts.

I will not make age an issue in this campaign. I am not going to exploit, for political purposes, my opponent's youth and inexperience.

Governments have a tendency not to solve problems, only to rearrange them.

Government exists to protect us from each other. We can't afford the government it would take to protect us from ourselves.

I used to say that politics was the second-oldest profession. I have come to know that it bears a gross similarity to the first.

Trust the people—this is the crucial lesson of history.

What I'd really like to do is go down in history as the President who made Americans believe in themselves again.

The current tax code is like a daily mugging.

Even Albert Einstein reportedly needed help on his 1040 form.

The taxpayer—that's someone who works for the federal government but doesn't have to take a civil-service exam.

If I could paraphrase a well-known statement by Will Rogers that he never met a man he didn't like—I'm afraid we have some people around here who never met a tax they didn't hike.

In the past two decades, we have created hundreds of new programs to provide personal assistance. Many of these programs may have come from a good heart, but not all have come from a clear head.

Inflation is as violent as a mugger, as frightening as an armed robber and as deadly as a hit man.

I have always stated that the nearest thing to eternal life we'll ever see on this earth is a government program.

Government is not the solution, it's the problem.

Our Constitution is to be celebrated not for being old, but for being young.

The Soviet Union would remain a one-party nation even if an opposition party were permitted—because everyone would join that party.

The one thing our Founding Fathers could not foresee—they were farmers, professional men, businessmen giving of their time and effort to an idea that became a country—was a nation governed by professional politicians who had a vested interest in getting re-elected. They probably envisioned a fellow serving a couple of hitches and then eagerly looking forward to getting back to the farm.

The very key to our success has been our ability, first and foremost among nations, to preserve our lasting values by making change work for us rather than against us.

Regimes planted by bayonets do not take root.

Nations do not mistrust each other because they are armed; they are armed because they mistrust each other.

No nation that placed its faith in parchment paper, while at the same time it gave up its protective hardware, ever lasted long enough to write many pages in history.

The Chinese philosopher, Sun Tzu, 2,500 years ago said winning a hundred victories in a hundred battles is not the acme of skill; to subdue the enemy without fighting is the acme of skill.

My fellow Americans: I'm pleased to tell you that I've signed legislation that will outlaw Russia forever. We begin bombing in five minutes. *[words spoken while testing a microphone, August 11, 1984]*

Since I came to the White House I got two hearing aids, a colon operation, skin cancer, and a prostate operation and I was shot. The damn thing is, I've never felt better in my life.

Education is not the means of showing people how to get what they want. Education is an exercise by means of which enough men, it is hoped, will learn to want what is worth having.

America is too great for small dreams.

Whoever would understand in his heart the meaning of America will find it in the life of Abraham Lincoln.

We are a nation that has a government—not the other way around. And that makes us special among the nations of the earth.

Remember the flap when I said, "We begin bombing in five minutes"? Remember when I fell asleep during my audience with the Pope? Remember Bitburg? Boy, those were the good old days.

George Herbert Walker Bush
Born June 12, 1924 ★ 41st President, 1989–1993
★ Republican

If anyone tells you that America's best days are behind her, they're looking the wrong way.

This is a fact: Strength in the pursuit of peace is no vice; isolation in the pursuit of security is no virtue.

America is never wholly herself unless she is engaged in high moral principle. We as a people have such a purpose today. It is to make kinder the face of the nation and gentler the face of the world.

This is America . . . a brilliant diversity spread like stars. Like a thousand points of light in a broad and peaceful sky.

I have spoken of a thousand points of light—of all the community organizations that are spread like stars throughout the nation, doing good. The old ideas are new again because they are not old, they are timeless: duty, sacrifice, commitment, and a patriotism that finds its expression in taking part and pitching in.

My opponent won't rule out raising taxes. But I will. And the Congress will push me to raise taxes, and I'll say no, and they'll push again and I'll say to them, read my lips, no new taxes.

The notion of political correctness has ignited controversy across the land. And although the movement arises from the laudable desire to sweep away the debris of racism and sexism and hatred, it replaces old prejudices with new ones. . . . What began as a crusade for civility has soured into a cause of conflict and even censorship.

Communism died this year. . . . The biggest thing that has happened in the world in my life, in our lives, is this: By the grace of God, America won the cold war.

William Jefferson Clinton
Born August 19, 1946 ★ 42nd President, 1993–2001 ★ Democrat

I want a leaner, not a meaner, government.

There is nothing wrong in America that can't be fixed with what is right in America.

Just as freedom has a price, it also has a purpose, and its name is progress.

The future is not an inheritance, it is an opportunity and an obligation.

The best social program is a good job.

I did not run for this job just to warm the seat. I desperately want to make a difference.

I refuse to be part of a generation that celebrates the death of communism abroad with the loss of the American dream at home.

Each generation of Americans must define what it means to be an American.

Profound and powerful forces are shaking and remaking our world. And the urgent question of our time is whether we can make change our friend and not our enemy.

The price of doing the same old thing is far higher than the price of change.

The world wars are over. The cold war has been won. Now it is our job to win the peace.

Politics is about economics. People forget that the New Deal was an economic program. A lot of social good came out of it, but it was an economic program.

The real American heroes today are the citizens who get up every morning and have the courage to work hard and play by the rules.

We must do what America does best: offer more opportunity to all and demand more responsibility from all.

Education is about more than making money and mastering technology, even in the twenty-first century. It's about making connections and mastering the complexities of the world. It's about seeing the world as it is and advancing the cause of human dignity.

This is the only country in the world where teenagers can have assault weapons designed only to kill other people, and use them with abandon on the streets of our cities. We can do better than that.

For too long we've been told about "us" and "them." Each and every election we see a new slate of arguments and ads telling us that "they" are the problem, not "us." But there can be no "them" in America. There's only us.

Instead of having shrill voices of discord, we need a chorus of harmony. In a chorus of harmony you know there are lots of differences, but you can hear all the voices.

I do not believe we can repair the basic fabric of society until people who are willing to work have work. Work organizes life. It gives structure and discipline to life. It gives meaning and self-esteem to people who are parents. It gives a role model to children.

[on White House life] I don't know whether it's

the finest public housing in America or the crown jewel of prison life. It's a very isolating life.

[on being diagnosed with laryngitis] My doctor ordered me to shut up, which will make every American happy.

[remarking on the reception to his lengthy speech at the 1988 Democratic Convention] It wasn't my finest hour. It wasn't even my finest hour and a half.

When I was in England I experimented with marijuana a time or two, and I didn't like it, and I didn't inhale, and I never tried it again.

I don't suppose there's any public figure that's ever been subject to any more violent personal attacks than I have.

If you live long enough, you'll make mistakes. But if you learn from them, you'll be a better person. It's how you handle adversity, not how it affects you. The main thing is never quit, never quit, never quit.

George Walker Bush
Born July 6, 1946 ★ 43rd President, 2001–present ★ Republican

You know what's interesting about Washington? It's the kind of place where second-guessing has become second nature.

[on cloning] Life is creation, not a commodity.

When an 18-year-old Palestinian girl is induced to blow herself up and in the process kills a 17-year-old Israeli girl, the future itself is dying . . .

Terrorism against our nation will not stand.

The pictures of airplanes flying into buildings, fires burning, huge structures collapsing, have filled us with disbelief, terrible sadness, and a quiet unyielding anger. These acts of mass murder were intended to frighten our nation into chaos and retreat. But they have failed; our country is strong.

Whether we bring our enemies to justice, or bring justice to our enemies, justice will be done. . . . Freedom and fear are at war. The advance of human freedom—the great achievement of our time, and the great hope of every time—now depends on us. Our nation—this generation—will lift a dark threat of violence from our people and our future. We will rally the world to this cause by our efforts, by our courage. We will not tire, we will not falter, and we will not fail.

Index